The Fearless Journeys of Marco Polo: A Traveler Ahead of His Time

Historical Books For Kids, Volume 15

Anam Rasheed

Published by Anam Rasheed, 2025.

While every precaution has been taken in the preparation of this book, the publisher assumes no responsibility for errors or omissions, or for damages resulting from the use of the information contained herein.

THE FEARLESS JOURNEYS OF MARCO POLO: A TRAVELER AHEAD OF HIS TIME

First edition. March 6, 2025.

Copyright © 2025 Anam Rasheed.

ISBN: 979-8230901181

Written by Anam Rasheed.

Table of Contents

Prologue..1
Chapter 1: A Young Boy with Big Dreams 2
Chapter 2: Setting Sail for the Unknown....................................4
Chapter 3: Across the Silk Road 8
Chapter 4: The Wonders of the Persian Empire 12
Chapter 5: Surviving the Harsh Deserts...................................16
Chapter 6: Meeting the Mongol Warriors 20
Chapter 7: Entering the Court of Kublai Khan........................24
Chapter 8: A Friendship with the Great Khan 28
Chapter 9: Exploring the Riches of China...............................32
Chapter 10: The Secrets of Paper Money.................................37
Chapter 11: Adventures in the Forbidden City.......................41
Chapter 12: Spices and Treasures of the East 45
Chapter 13: A Journey to the Land of Gold............................49
Chapter 14: Facing Dangers on the Road 53
Chapter 15: The Long Voyage Back Home..............................57
Chapter 16: A Stranger in His Own Land...............................61
Chapter 17: Sharing Tales of the East 65
Chapter 18: The Book That Shocked Europe..........................69
Chapter 19: Doubters and Believers 74
Chapter 20: The Legacy of a Great Explorer 78
Epilogue..82

Prologue

Imagine a time before airplanes, trains, or even reliable maps. A time when much of the world was a mystery, filled with lands few had ever seen and stories that seemed too incredible to be true. This was the world Marco Polo was born into—a world ready to be explored by those brave enough to face the unknown.

In the 13th century, most Europeans knew little about the distant lands of the East. They had heard whispers of powerful emperors, golden cities, and spices worth more than gold. But only a handful dared to venture beyond familiar borders to see these wonders for themselves. Marco Polo was one of them.

Born in Venice, Italy, Marco grew up in a city buzzing with trade. Ships arrived daily with goods from distant lands—silks from China, spices from India, and jewels from Persia. But Marco wanted to see these places with his own eyes. He dreamed of adventure, of meeting kings and emperors, of discovering the secrets of lands far beyond his home.

At just seventeen years old, Marco set out with his father and uncle on a journey that would change his life—and the world—forever. He would travel thousands of miles across deserts, mountains, and mighty rivers. He would stand before Kublai Khan, the ruler of the vast Mongol Empire, and explore the wonders of China. He would return home with stories that many refused to believe.

This is the tale of Marco Polo, the boy who became one of history's greatest explorers. His fearless journeys opened the eyes of Europe to a world they had never imagined. Now, it's your turn to travel with Marco and discover the wonders of his incredible adventure.

Chapter 1: A Young Boy with Big Dreams

Marco Polo was not born into a life of adventure, but he was born into a family that knew all about it. He came into the world in the year 1254, in the city of Venice, Italy. Venice was a powerful place back then, full of sailors, traders, and merchants who traveled across the seas to buy and sell goods. It was a city of sparkling canals instead of streets, with boats gliding through the water like carriages. The air was always filled with the scent of spices, fresh fish, and the sounds of merchants calling out their latest treasures from distant lands.

Marco's father, Niccolò Polo, and his uncle, Maffeo, were both merchants who spent their lives sailing across the Mediterranean Sea and beyond, trading silk, jewels, spices, and gold. They had already gone on an extraordinary journey to faraway lands even before Marco was born. But Marco didn't know any of this when he was just a small boy. He didn't meet his father until he was about 15 years old because Niccolò was away on an adventure when Marco was born and didn't return until many years later. Growing up without a father, Marco was raised by his extended family. He spent his childhood wandering the streets of Venice, watching the great ships come in, listening to the stories of sailors who had been to lands he could only dream of, and wondering what lay beyond the horizon.

Even though Marco was just a boy, he had a mind full of curiosity. He wanted to know more about the world, not just from stories but by seeing it for himself. He loved listening to travelers describe lands where golden temples touched the sky, where strange animals roamed, and where spices grew so rare and valuable that they were worth more than gold. He imagined himself walking through deserts, riding across mountains, and standing before the palaces of great kings. His dreams were filled with adventure, but he never expected that one day, he would get the chance to live them.

When his father and uncle returned to Venice after their long journey, they brought back incredible tales of the Mongol Empire, a vast kingdom ruled by the mighty Kublai Khan, the grandson of Genghis Khan. They spoke of cities larger than any in Europe, of people wearing silks so fine they felt like water, and of riches beyond imagination. The Mongol Empire stretched across much of Asia, and its great leader, Kublai Khan, was eager to learn about the lands of the West. He had even given the Polo brothers a message for the Pope, asking for wise men to come to his court.

Hearing these stories, Marco was captivated. He couldn't believe that such wonders existed outside of Venice. He wanted more than anything to see these lands for himself. He had grown up in a city filled with traders, but he had never left its borders. Now, with his father and uncle planning another trip, he saw his chance. Even though it was dangerous, even though the journey would take years, Marco was ready. He wasn't just a boy anymore—he was a young adventurer in the making.

At just 17 years old, Marco Polo set out on the greatest journey of his life. He was leaving behind everything he had ever known—his home, his family, his comfortable life in Venice—to travel across deserts, mountains, and foreign lands he had never seen. He had no idea what awaited him, no idea how long he would be gone, and no idea that his journey would make him one of the most famous explorers in history. But none of that mattered. All that mattered was that he was finally about to see the world with his own eyes.

The road ahead would be long, filled with challenges, dangers, and wonders beyond imagination. But for Marco, the adventure had only just begun.

Chapter 2: Setting Sail for the Unknown

When Marco Polo set out on his journey in 1271, he was about to leave behind everything familiar—his home in Venice, the bustling markets filled with merchants shouting about silk and spices, the canals that carried boats instead of wagons, and the comforts of a city he had known all his life. But he wasn't just going on a short trip. He was about to embark on an adventure that would take him farther than most people had ever traveled. He didn't know how long he would be gone, what dangers he would face, or what incredible sights he would see. The only thing he knew for sure was that the journey ahead would change his life forever.

Marco was traveling with his father, Niccolò, and his uncle, Maffeo, two experienced merchants who had already visited distant lands. They had been to the powerful Mongol Empire and met its great ruler, Kublai Khan, the grandson of the fearsome Genghis Khan. The Khan had been fascinated by the Western world and wanted to know more about it. He had even given the Polo brothers a special request: to bring back intelligent men who could teach him about Christianity and European culture. So, when they set off on their second journey, this time with young Marco, they carried letters from the Pope, gifts, and precious trade goods to present to the mighty ruler of the Mongols.

Their journey began with a sea voyage. Venice, being a city of canals and waterways, was filled with expert sailors and traders who navigated the Mediterranean Sea with ease. Marco must have felt a thrill of excitement as he stepped onto the ship, the salty sea air filling his lungs and the cries of seagulls echoing above. As the ship set sail, he watched as the familiar sights of Venice slowly disappeared in the distance. Ahead of him lay lands he had only heard about in stories.

The first part of their journey took them to Acre, a major trading port in the Middle East, in what is now modern-day Israel. Here, they had to wait for the Pope's response to Kublai Khan's request. However, instead of getting a group of wise men to travel with them, they received only two friars. Unfortunately, these friars became too frightened of the dangerous journey ahead and soon turned back. This left Marco, his father, and his uncle to continue the adventure on their own.

From Acre, they traveled inland to the Persian Empire (modern-day Iran), a land of vast deserts, towering mountains, and great cities filled with scholars, traders, and warriors. This was a place of ancient wisdom, where people studied the stars, created intricate art, and wrote poetry about kings and heroes. Marco must have marveled at the golden domes of Persian palaces, the grand mosques where prayers echoed, and the busy markets filled with carpets, jewelry, and exotic foods.

But traveling through Persia was not easy. The Polo family had to cross treacherous deserts where the sun blazed down like fire during the day and the cold winds howled at night. There were times when they had to ration water, carefully sipping only what was necessary to survive. They had to avoid bandits—dangerous groups of thieves who roamed the trade routes, waiting to attack travelers carrying valuable goods. Marco, still a teenager, was learning firsthand how unpredictable and perilous the world could be.

After months of crossing dry, dusty lands, the travelers reached the city of Hormuz, a major port on the Persian Gulf. Here, they hoped to find a ship that could take them across the sea toward India and China. But the ships they found were poorly built and unsafe for such a long journey. Instead of risking their lives at sea, they decided to continue overland, following the ancient Silk Road, a network of trade routes that connected Europe to the vast lands of Asia.

As they moved deeper into the unknown, Marco saw sights that few Europeans had ever witnessed. He encountered people with different customs, languages, and traditions. He watched in amazement as camels, known as the "ships of the desert," carried heavy loads across endless stretches of sand. He tasted strange new foods, from spicy dishes made with ingredients he had never seen before to sweet fruits that burst with flavor. He met traders who carried silk so fine it shimmered in the sunlight, and he saw glass, porcelain, and rare jewels that were worth a fortune.

But the journey was far from easy. At times, the roads were nothing more than rough paths through towering mountains where the air was thin and breathing became difficult. At other times, they had to cross dangerous rivers, carefully guiding their animals through rushing waters. They had to be constantly alert, for wild animals, thieves, and sudden storms could make a single mistake deadly. Yet, through all these challenges, Marco's spirit remained unbroken. He was no longer just a boy from Venice—he was becoming a true explorer.

For three long years, Marco and his family traveled through lands few Europeans had ever seen. They moved through the towering peaks of the Pamir Mountains, where the cold was bitter and the wind howled through the valleys. They journeyed through the mighty Gobi Desert, where the endless dunes stretched as far as the eye could see, and the sun beat down with an unrelenting heat. At night, under a sky filled with stars, Marco must have wondered what else lay ahead.

Finally, after thousands of miles, after braving deserts, mountains, and wild landscapes, they reached the lands of the Mongol Empire. The closer they got to the heart of Kublai Khan's domain, the more Marco realized he was entering a world unlike anything he had ever imagined. Great walled cities rose up from the horizon, filled with people dressed in brightly colored robes. Markets bustled with activity as merchants sold spices, pearls, jade, and rare fabrics. Palaces shimmered in the distance, guarded by warriors on horseback who could shoot arrows with incredible precision.

Marco had set sail for the unknown, and now he had arrived at the most powerful empire of his time. The young boy from Venice, who once only dreamed of adventure, was about to meet the ruler of one of the greatest civilizations in history. But his journey was far from over. In fact, it was just beginning.

Chapter 3: Across the Silk Road

The Silk Road was one of the most famous and mysterious trade routes in history, stretching across vast lands filled with deserts, mountains, and ancient cities. It was not a single road but a network of paths connecting Europe and Asia, allowing traders, travelers, and explorers to exchange goods, ideas, and cultures. It was along this legendary route that Marco Polo, his father Niccolò, and his uncle Maffeo journeyed on their way to meet the great Kublai Khan. This was a road filled with wonders, dangers, and discoveries, and Marco, just a young man at the time, would experience it all firsthand.

Setting off from Venice in 1271, Marco Polo and his family made their way through the Mediterranean, stopping in Acre and then moving across Persia (modern-day Iran). By the time they reached the edge of the Persian lands, they knew that the most difficult part of their journey lay ahead. The Silk Road was not an easy path to travel. It was a road filled with challenges—towering mountains, scorching deserts, and dangerous thieves who lurked along the way, waiting to attack merchants carrying valuable goods. But it was also the road that connected the greatest civilizations on Earth, bringing together the cultures of Europe, the Middle East, Central Asia, India, and China.

As Marco Polo traveled deeper into the Silk Road, he encountered places and people unlike anything he had seen before. He passed through bustling trade cities where merchants from many lands gathered to sell their treasures. These markets were filled with silk so fine it shimmered in the sunlight, spices that filled the air with exotic scents, and rare jewels that glittered like the stars. Marco must have watched in amazement as traders from different cultures bartered and exchanged goods, speaking in dozens of languages, each one carrying knowledge and stories from their distant homelands.

But beyond the markets, the real challenges of the Silk Road began. One of the first great obstacles Marco and his family faced was the towering Pamir Mountains, known as the "Roof of the World." These mountains were among the highest in the world, with steep, rocky paths, freezing temperatures, and thin air that made every step exhausting. Travelers had to be careful not to slip on the icy trails, and their pack animals—strong horses and camels—struggled to carry their heavy loads over the rough terrain. At night, the temperatures dropped so low that Marco and his companions had to huddle together for warmth. Despite the challenges, Marco was fascinated by the beauty of the mountains. He saw deep valleys covered in snow, rivers cutting through the rocky cliffs, and eagles soaring high above the peaks. He also encountered people who lived in these harsh lands—shepherds who knew the mountains better than anyone, guiding travelers through the safest paths.

After weeks of struggling through the mountains, the Polo family descended into the great Taklamakan Desert, one of the most dangerous deserts in the world. Unlike the soft, rolling dunes of other deserts, the Taklamakan was harsh and unforgiving. Its name meant "the place of no return," and many travelers feared getting lost in its endless sands. Marco and his family had to follow carefully planned routes, stopping at small oases where they could find water and shelter. The sun beat down mercilessly during the day, turning the sand into a blazing furnace, while at night, the temperatures dropped to near freezing. The wind howled across the dunes, sometimes whipping up powerful sandstorms that could bury entire caravans. Travelers had to cover their faces with cloth to keep the sand from getting into their mouths and eyes.

Despite the hardships, Marco was fascinated by the desert. He saw strange mirages—optical illusions that made it look like lakes of water shimmered in the distance, only to disappear upon approach. He listened to the legends of the desert, including stories of ghostly voices calling out to travelers, leading them astray. He also encountered nomadic tribes who had learned to survive in the harsh environment, moving from one oasis to another and trading goods with passing caravans.

Beyond the desert, Marco and his family entered the lands of Central Asia, where they discovered the mighty cities of the Silk Road. One of the most magnificent was Samarkand, a city that dazzled Marco with its grand palaces, towering mosques, and vibrant markets. Here, he saw scholars studying astronomy, mathematics, and medicine, recording their knowledge in beautiful books with intricate designs. Marco also witnessed the wealth of the region—golden domes shining under the sun, fountains flowing with fresh water, and rulers dressed in robes of silk and embroidered patterns.

As they continued their journey, they passed through more legendary cities, each one a meeting point for different cultures and ideas. Marco observed how Chinese traders brought porcelain and paper money, while Indian merchants carried precious gems and spices. Arabian traders introduced perfumes, glassware, and knowledge from the great scholars of the Islamic world. The Silk Road was not just about trade—it was about sharing discoveries, languages, and inventions.

Traveling along the Silk Road also meant encountering different rulers and local warlords. Some were kind and welcomed travelers with open arms, offering food, shelter, and protection. Others were dangerous, demanding high taxes or threatening those who passed through their lands. The Polo family had to be cautious, making sure to show respect to every leader they met. They carried gifts and letters from European rulers, which helped them earn the trust of those in power.

After years of travel, enduring harsh deserts, freezing mountains, and endless stretches of road, Marco and his family finally reached the eastern end of the Silk Road—the mighty empire of Kublai Khan. They arrived at Shangdu, also known as Xanadu, the Khan's summer palace, where they would be welcomed into the heart of one of the most powerful empires the world had ever seen. Marco had set out as a young boy with dreams of adventure, and now he had traveled farther than almost any European before him.

The Silk Road had been more than just a route—it had been a journey through the wonders of the world. It had shown Marco sights he never imagined, introduced him to people from distant lands, and tested his courage through hardships he had never known. But his journey was far from over. He was about to step into the court of the great Kublai Khan, where even greater adventures awaited him.

Chapter 4: The Wonders of the Persian Empire

As Marco Polo and his family traveled eastward along the Silk Road, one of the most incredible places they encountered was the mighty Persian Empire. Persia, which today is known as Iran, was a land of great wealth, wisdom, and power. It was home to vast deserts, towering mountains, lush green valleys, and cities filled with grand palaces, bustling markets, and towering mosques. The Persian Empire was one of the most advanced civilizations of its time, known for its rich history, incredible inventions, and breathtaking art and architecture. Marco, who had never seen such a land before, was captivated by the wonders of Persia.

The cities of Persia were like jewels scattered across the desert, each one offering something unique and fascinating. As Marco entered these cities, he found himself surrounded by magnificent buildings made of marble, decorated with colorful tiles that shimmered in the sunlight. These tiles were arranged in intricate geometric patterns, creating dazzling designs on mosques, palaces, and courtyards. Persian architects were famous for their skill, and their buildings had towering domes, elegant arches, and beautiful fountains that made the cities feel like something out of a dream.

One of the most famous cities Marco visited was Tabriz, a major center of trade and culture. Here, the streets were filled with merchants selling goods from all over the world. Spices from India, silk from China, gold and silver from Europe, and rare jewels from faraway lands all passed through Tabriz. The city had a massive bazaar, a marketplace where traders gathered to buy and sell their goods. The scent of exotic spices filled the air, and Marco watched as merchants carefully weighed and measured rare powders that could add flavor to food or be used in medicine.

Persia was also a land of scholars and poets. The people of Persia highly valued knowledge, and they had great libraries filled with books on science, mathematics, astronomy, and medicine. Persian scholars had made many discoveries about the stars and planets, and they used advanced mathematical calculations to predict celestial events. They also had skilled doctors who knew how to treat diseases using herbal medicines, a practice that was far ahead of its time.

One of the most famous Persian poets was Rumi, whose poetry was known for its deep wisdom and beautiful language. Persian poetry was often written in elegant calligraphy, a type of artistic handwriting that turned words into a form of art. Marco must have been amazed by the beauty of Persian books, which were not just sources of knowledge but also decorated masterpieces, with golden letters, detailed illustrations, and delicate designs along the borders of each page.

Another incredible city that Marco and his family passed through was Yazd, located in the heart of the desert. Unlike other cities, Yazd had developed a unique way to survive in the harsh desert environment. The people of Yazd built special wind towers, known as "badgirs," which worked as natural air conditioners, capturing the wind and cooling down the buildings. These wind towers allowed the city to stay cool even in the scorching heat of the desert. Marco had never seen anything like it before, and he marveled at how the Persians had found clever ways to adapt to their surroundings.

Persian culture was also famous for its luxurious textiles and carpets. Persian rugs were known throughout the world for their beauty and craftsmanship. These carpets were made by hand, with weavers carefully knotting each thread to create breathtaking designs filled with flowers, animals, and geometric shapes. Wealthy families and rulers often decorated their palaces with these fine carpets, and Marco saw firsthand the incredible skill that went into making them.

But Persia was not just a land of beauty and wisdom—it was also a land of power. The Persian Empire had once been ruled by great kings who controlled vast territories stretching across the Middle East and Central Asia. Even though the Mongols had taken control of Persia by the time Marco visited, the influence of Persian culture remained strong. Persian warriors were known for their skill in battle, and Marco learned about their famous cavalry, soldiers who rode on horseback with great speed and agility. These warriors were experts with bows and swords, able to strike their enemies with incredible precision.

One of the most breathtaking sights Marco encountered in Persia was the grand palaces of the ruling class. These palaces were decorated with gold, silver, and precious gems. Some had beautiful courtyards filled with fountains, where water flowed smoothly through stone channels, creating peaceful gardens in the middle of the desert. Persian rulers loved luxury, and their homes were filled with silk cushions, golden goblets, and delicate porcelain dishes brought from China.

The food of Persia was another wonder that fascinated Marco. Persian cuisine was rich in flavors, using a variety of spices, herbs, and dried fruits to create delicious dishes. He tasted kebabs, flavorful rice dishes, and sweet desserts made with honey and nuts. One of the most famous Persian foods was saffron rice, a dish made with one of the most expensive spices in the world. Saffron, which comes from a special flower, was so valuable that it was sometimes worth more than gold.

Marco also learned about the Persian tradition of storytelling. Persian storytellers, known as "naqqals," would gather in marketplaces or palace courtyards and recite epic tales of heroes, kings, and mythical creatures. One of the most famous stories Marco may have heard was from the "Shahnameh," an epic poem that told the history of Persia's greatest rulers and warriors. These stories were filled with bravery, adventure, and magical events, much like Marco's own journey across the Silk Road.

Another important part of Persian culture was its religion. Many Persians followed Islam, and Marco saw the great mosques where people gathered to pray. The mosques were decorated with beautiful calligraphy, and their towering minarets stood high above the cities. But Persia was also home to one of the oldest religions in the world—Zoroastrianism. Marco may have visited the famous Fire Temples, where a sacred flame burned continuously, believed to have been kept alive for centuries as a symbol of purity and wisdom.

As Marco continued his journey through Persia, he realized that this was a land unlike any other. It was a place of great knowledge, breathtaking art, powerful rulers, and skilled merchants. Every city had its own unique character, from the bustling trade centers to the quiet desert settlements. The people of Persia had mastered the art of living in harmony with their environment, creating incredible cities and inventions that made life easier and more beautiful.

By the time Marco Polo and his family left Persia, they had seen wonders beyond their imagination. But their journey was far from over. Ahead of them lay even greater challenges—the vast deserts of Central Asia, the towering peaks of the Pamir Mountains, and the legendary lands of the Mongol Empire. Marco had been amazed by the splendor of Persia, but he knew that even greater adventures awaited him. He was not just a traveler anymore—he was an explorer, discovering the mysteries of the world one step at a time.

Chapter 5: Surviving the Harsh Deserts

Traveling through the deserts of the Silk Road was one of the most difficult and dangerous challenges that Marco Polo and his family faced on their journey to the East. These vast, empty lands stretched for hundreds of miles, with no signs of life except for the occasional oasis, where travelers could find water and shelter. The deserts were scorching hot during the day, with the sun blazing down like a fiery torch, and freezing cold at night, with winds that cut through even the thickest cloaks. Sandstorms could appear out of nowhere, swallowing everything in their path, and mirages—false images of water shimmering in the distance—could trick even the most experienced travelers. To survive the harsh deserts, Marco and his companions had to rely on careful planning, expert guides, and the strength of their camels, which were the lifeline of any desert journey.

One of the first great deserts Marco Polo encountered was the Iranian Plateau, a dry and rocky land that stretched across Persia. Unlike the soft dunes of the Arabian Desert, this area was filled with sharp stones, jagged cliffs, and dry riverbeds that made travel slow and difficult. Marco and his family had to be careful with their supplies, carrying enough water and food to last for weeks. Water was more precious than gold in the desert, and travelers stored it in animal skins or clay jars, carefully rationing each drop. They traveled in caravans—large groups of merchants, traders, and guides—because crossing the desert alone was almost certain death. If a person got lost, there was little chance of survival. The heat could cause extreme thirst, and without water, a person could collapse within hours.

As they moved eastward, Marco and his companions reached one of the most feared deserts in the world—the great Taklamakan Desert. Its name meant "the place of no return," and for good reason. It was a vast sea of shifting sands, where the wind constantly moved the dunes, erasing paths and landmarks. The Taklamakan was a silent, lifeless world where nothing seemed to grow, and the only sound was the whisper of the wind. Many travelers believed the desert was haunted, saying that at night, they could hear ghostly voices calling their names, leading them astray. These sounds were actually the wind sweeping across the dunes, but to tired and frightened travelers, they seemed like spirits of the lost.

To survive in the Taklamakan, Marco and his fellow travelers followed ancient caravan routes, moving from one oasis to another. These small patches of green were the only places where water could be found, and they were essential for survival. Some oases were surrounded by palm trees, with cool, clear pools of water, while others had small villages where people had learned to live in harmony with the desert. These people, known as the Uighurs, were skilled traders and expert desert guides. They knew how to find hidden wells and how to navigate by the stars at night. They taught Marco that traveling during the heat of the day was dangerous, so instead, caravans often moved at dawn or dusk, when the air was cooler.

Camels were the most important animals in the desert, and Marco learned to appreciate their incredible ability to survive in such harsh conditions. Known as the "ships of the desert," camels could travel for days without drinking water, storing fat in their humps to keep them going. Their thick eyelashes and nostrils could close to protect them from sandstorms, and their wide, padded feet prevented them from sinking into the soft sand. Camels carried supplies, goods for trade, and even weary travelers who could not walk any further. However, they were not always the easiest animals to handle. They could be stubborn, making loud groaning noises when forced to move, and sometimes they would refuse to get up if they were overloaded. Marco must have watched in amusement as caravan drivers tried to coax their camels forward, using special calls and gentle nudges.

But camels alone were not enough to guarantee survival. Marco and his companions had to be prepared for the many dangers of the desert. One of the greatest threats was the sandstorm. These storms could rise suddenly, with strong winds lifting the sand into the air, creating blinding clouds that could last for hours. Travelers caught in a sandstorm had to cover their faces with cloth to avoid breathing in the fine dust. Sometimes, the only way to survive was to stop moving, huddle close together, and wait for the storm to pass.

Another danger was the lack of food. In the desert, there were no crops, no rivers filled with fish, and few animals to hunt. Travelers had to bring dried meat, nuts, dates, and hard bread that could last for weeks without spoiling. Some carried small bags of rice or grains, which could be cooked when water was available. Marco also learned about a special drink called fermented mare's milk, made from horse's milk, which was popular among the Mongols and desert nomads. It was sour but nutritious, providing energy for long journeys.

Despite the hardships, the desert had a beauty of its own. At night, the sky was a blanket of stars, shining more brightly than Marco had ever seen in Venice. The silence of the desert was almost magical, with no city noise, only the occasional cry of a distant bird or the gentle creaking of camel saddles. Some nights, Marco and his companions would sit around a small fire, listening to the tales of other travelers. Stories of lost cities buried beneath the sand, hidden treasures guarded by desert spirits, and brave explorers who had crossed the endless dunes filled the air.

One of the most fascinating places Marco encountered in the desert was the Lop Nor region, an area filled with strange landscapes. Here, the ground was cracked and dry, with salt flats stretching as far as the eye could see. The heat made the air shimmer, creating illusions of water where there was none. It was easy to see why so many travelers were fooled by mirages, wandering toward an imaginary lake only to find themselves deeper in the wasteland. Marco learned to trust his guides and never chase after what seemed too good to be true.

Another desert Marco crossed was the Gobi Desert, which was different from the Taklamakan. Unlike the endless sand dunes of the Taklamakan, the Gobi was filled with rocky plains, dry grasslands, and even occasional patches of snow in the colder months. The Gobi had wild animals that survived despite the harsh conditions, including wild horses, small desert foxes, and even camels that had adapted to life without much water. The Gobi was also home to the Mongol tribes, who lived in large tents called yurts, made from felt and wood. These nomads were skilled horse riders, and Marco was amazed by their ability to travel great distances across the desert without losing their way.

After months of crossing deserts, Marco and his family finally reached the more fertile lands of China, where rivers flowed, crops grew, and cities flourished. The harsh deserts had tested their strength, forcing them to endure extreme temperatures, long days of endless walking, and the constant challenge of finding food and water. But they had survived, thanks to careful planning, strong camels, and the wisdom of the desert people who had guided them.

Looking back, Marco must have realized that crossing the desert was one of the greatest adventures of his journey. It was a place of hardship, mystery, and beauty, where only the strongest and smartest travelers could survive. He had seen landscapes that seemed otherworldly, met people whose way of life was entirely different from his own, and learned the skills needed to travel in one of the most unforgiving environments on Earth. The deserts of the Silk Road were not just obstacles to overcome—they were an essential part of the journey, shaping Marco into the legendary explorer he would become.

Chapter 6: Meeting the Mongol Warriors

As Marco Polo and his companions traveled deeper into Asia, they entered lands ruled by one of the most powerful and feared groups in history—the Mongol warriors. These fierce horsemen had built a vast empire that stretched across Asia and into Europe, conquering lands with incredible speed and skill. They were known for their unmatched ability to ride horses, their deadly accuracy with bows and arrows, and their disciplined way of life. But beyond their reputation as fearless fighters, the Mongols also had a rich culture, a complex system of government, and a deep sense of loyalty to their leader, the Great Khan. Meeting the Mongol warriors would be one of the most fascinating and eye-opening experiences of Marco Polo's journey.

Marco and his family first began hearing stories about the Mongols while traveling along the Silk Road. Merchants, travelers, and local villagers all spoke of these warriors with a mixture of admiration and fear. Some told tales of entire cities surrendering to the Mongols without a fight because they knew resistance was useless. Others described how the Mongols could ride for days without stopping, living off dried meat and fermented mare's milk, and how their archers could hit a target from hundreds of feet away while galloping at full speed. These stories made Marco even more eager to see the Mongols with his own eyes.

As they ventured further east, they finally encountered a group of Mongol warriors. At first, Marco must have felt a mix of excitement and fear. The warriors wore heavy fur-lined coats, strong leather boots, and helmets made of iron or hardened leather. Their faces were weathered from years of riding in the harsh winds of the open plains, and they carried weapons that looked deadly even from a distance—curved swords, long spears, and bows with arrows that could pierce armor. Despite their fearsome appearance, the Mongols were not just brutal fighters. They lived by a strict code of honor and loyalty, and they welcomed travelers who showed respect.

Marco soon learned that the Mongols' greatest weapon was not their swords or arrows, but their horses. Each warrior had several horses, switching from one to another when a horse grew tired. This allowed them to travel incredible distances without slowing down. Mongol horses were small but strong, able to survive on little food and water. A warrior could ride for hours without stopping, even sleeping in the saddle while his horse kept moving. Marco must have watched in amazement as the Mongols demonstrated their famous riding skills, twisting and turning in the saddle, firing arrows in every direction without losing balance.

One of the most surprising things Marco discovered was how well-organized the Mongols were. They did not fight in chaotic battles like some armies. Instead, they used clever tactics, dividing their forces into small, highly skilled groups that could attack from multiple directions. They used signals, such as flags and drums, to communicate across great distances, allowing their commanders to control the battle with precision. If they needed to cross a river, they would tie their supplies to leather bags filled with air, using them as floating rafts. They were not only warriors but also expert strategists who planned their battles carefully.

Despite their reputation for being fierce in battle, the Mongols were also surprisingly disciplined. They followed strict laws set by their leader, the Great Khan. Stealing, lying, or disobeying orders was not tolerated, and punishment was swift. They believed in loyalty above all else, and every warrior was expected to obey his commander without question. If a warrior showed great bravery or skill, he could rise in rank regardless of his birth. Unlike in Europe, where noble families ruled over commoners, the Mongols valued ability more than bloodlines.

Marco also learned about their unique way of life. Unlike the people of Venice, who lived in grand stone houses, the Mongols lived in large, round tents called yurts. These tents were made of felt and could be packed up and moved whenever the tribe decided to travel. Inside a yurt, a fire burned in the center, keeping the space warm even in the freezing winters. The Mongols' diet was simple but provided them with energy—mostly meat, dairy products, and dried foods that could last for months. Marco tried fermented mare's milk, a drink called kumis, which was sour and slightly alcoholic. Though strange at first, it was a favorite among the Mongols and was believed to give strength to warriors.

The Mongols also had a unique postal system that allowed messages to travel across the vast empire at incredible speed. They set up relay stations with fresh horses every few miles, allowing messengers to switch to a new horse and continue riding without stopping. This system, called the Yam, was one of the fastest communication networks in the world at the time. Messages that would take weeks to travel by normal means could be delivered in just a few days. This was how the Great Khan kept control over his massive empire, always knowing what was happening in different regions.

Marco was especially fascinated by the way the Mongols trained their warriors from a young age. Boys as young as five or six learned to ride horses, and by the time they were teenagers, they could shoot arrows while riding at full speed. They practiced daily, competing in contests of strength, endurance, and accuracy. Marco watched as young Mongols raced their horses across the open plains, shot targets from incredible distances, and wrestled each other to prove their strength. These warriors were not just soldiers; they were raised to be fighters from birth, making them some of the most formidable opponents in history.

As Marco spent more time among the Mongols, he realized that they were not just warlike conquerors—they were also deeply connected to their traditions and beliefs. They respected nature, believing that the land, sky, and animals were all part of a great balance.

They performed rituals before battle, asking the spirits for guidance, and celebrated victories with great feasts. Music and storytelling were also important to them, and at night, warriors would sit around fires, sharing tales of past battles and heroic deeds.

Eventually, Marco and his companions were invited to meet the most powerful man in the Mongol Empire—the Great Khan himself. This was a rare honor, as few outsiders were allowed to enter the court of the Mongols' leader. But before reaching the Great Khan, Marco had already gained valuable knowledge about the Mongol warriors—how they lived, how they fought, and how they ruled over the largest empire the world had ever seen.

Meeting the Mongols was one of the most unforgettable parts of Marco Polo's journey. He had witnessed their strength, their discipline, and their deep-rooted traditions. He had seen how they built an empire not just through warfare, but through clever strategies, strict organization, and a powerful system of communication. These warriors were unlike any Marco had ever seen before, and their way of life left a lasting impression on him. As he continued his journey toward the court of the Great Khan, he carried with him the lessons he had learned from the fearless Mongol warriors, lessons that would shape his understanding of the world forever.

Chapter 7: Entering the Court of Kublai Khan

After months of grueling travel across deserts, mountains, and endless plains, Marco Polo and his companions finally arrived at the heart of the Mongol Empire—the magnificent court of Kublai Khan. It was a place unlike anything Marco had ever seen, filled with incredible sights, sounds, and wonders beyond his wildest imagination. This was not just a palace; it was the center of one of the largest and most powerful empires in history. Here, Marco would meet the Great Khan himself, a ruler who controlled lands stretching from China to the Middle East, from Russia to the borders of Europe. The journey had been long and dangerous, but now, standing at the gates of Kublai Khan's court, Marco knew he was about to witness something extraordinary.

As they approached the city, Marco saw the vast capital of the Mongol Empire—Khanbaliq, the city that would later become Beijing. Unlike the cities of Europe, with their narrow streets and stone buildings, Khanbaliq was vast and carefully designed. The city was surrounded by strong walls, protecting it from enemies, and inside, the streets were wide, organized, and bustling with life. Merchants from all over Asia, the Middle East, and even Europe came here to trade goods—silk, spices, gold, and rare treasures that Marco had never seen before. The marketplaces were filled with the scent of exotic foods, the sound of traders calling out their prices, and the sight of camels and carts carrying goods from distant lands. It was a city that felt alive, constantly moving, constantly changing.

At the heart of Khanbaliq stood the palace of Kublai Khan, a structure so grand that it left Marco speechless. The palace was surrounded by large gardens filled with rare flowers, fruit trees, and fountains that sparkled in the sunlight. Birds from far-off lands chirped in golden cages, and white marble pathways led to the grand entrance.

The palace itself was enormous, with golden rooftops that shone brightly under the sky. The walls were decorated with intricate designs, telling the story of the Mongol Empire's great conquests and victories. Everything about the palace spoke of wealth, power, and the greatness of its ruler.

Before meeting Kublai Khan, Marco and his family had to go through a series of rituals to show respect. The Mongols had strict customs, and anyone who entered the presence of the Great Khan had to follow them. First, they had to remove their weapons and kneel before the royal guards, who examined them closely. Then, they were led into a massive hall where dozens of important officials, generals, and noblemen waited. The atmosphere was serious and grand, with everyone dressed in luxurious silk robes, embroidered with gold and precious gems. The Mongol court was not only a place of power but also a place of art, music, and intelligence. Scholars, astronomers, and advisors from different parts of the empire were present, offering their wisdom to the Khan.

Finally, the moment came. Marco Polo was led into the audience chamber where Kublai Khan himself sat on a grand throne. The Great Khan was not just a fearsome warrior like his ancestors; he was a wise and intelligent ruler who valued knowledge and diplomacy. He was dressed in rich, flowing robes made of the finest silk, his belt decorated with dazzling jewels. He had a strong presence, with sharp eyes that seemed to see everything. Though he was a powerful emperor, he did not rely only on brute strength—he ruled with strategy, wisdom, and a deep understanding of different cultures.

Marco and his companions bowed deeply before Kublai Khan, showing the utmost respect. It was a moment of great significance—few Europeans had ever stood before the Great Khan, and even fewer had earned his trust. Marco's father and uncle, who had visited Kublai Khan years before, spoke first, presenting gifts they had brought from Venice. The Mongols respected the exchange of gifts as a sign of goodwill, and the Great Khan received them with interest. Then, he turned his attention to Marco.

At just 21 years old, Marco Polo was younger than most of the travelers who visited the Mongol court. But he had something that set him apart—his curiosity, his sharp mind, and his ability to observe and learn. Kublai Khan saw something special in him and decided to test his intelligence. The Great Khan asked Marco many questions about Venice, about Europe, and about the customs of the Western world. Marco, who had spent years traveling and learning about different cultures, answered with confidence. He described the cities of Italy, the great cathedrals, the markets filled with goods from across the Mediterranean, and the way European rulers governed their people. He also spoke about the latest advancements in technology, shipbuilding, and trade.

Kublai Khan was fascinated. He had always been eager to learn about the lands beyond his empire, and Marco's descriptions painted a vivid picture of a world the Mongols knew little about. The Great Khan listened carefully, nodding as Marco spoke. Unlike many rulers who only cared about war and conquest, Kublai Khan valued knowledge, trade, and diplomacy. He believed that ruling an empire as vast as his required more than just an army—it required wisdom and an understanding of different cultures.

As the days passed, Marco was invited to stay at the Mongol court. He was given fine clothes, delicious food, and the chance to see the inner workings of the empire. He witnessed grand ceremonies where gifts were brought from distant provinces, celebrations where dancers and musicians entertained the court, and official meetings where important decisions were made. He saw how Kublai Khan governed, listening to his advisors, sending messengers across the empire, and making plans to expand trade routes. Unlike the European rulers who relied on their noble families, Kublai Khan chose the most capable people to serve in his government, regardless of their background.

Marco was deeply impressed by this system, which allowed talented individuals from all over the empire to rise to important positions.

One of the most astonishing things Marco saw in Kublai Khan's court was the use of paper money. In Europe, people used gold, silver, and coins for trade, but here, the Mongols had developed a system where people used paper as currency. Marco watched in amazement as merchants exchanged these paper notes for goods, trusting that they held value. It was a revolutionary idea, and it showed just how advanced the Mongol Empire was in terms of economics and trade.

Marco also learned about the vast network of roads and postal stations that connected the empire. Kublai Khan had created a system where messengers on horseback could deliver messages across thousands of miles in record time. This allowed him to communicate with different parts of his empire quickly, keeping control over even the most distant regions. Marco was astonished by the efficiency of this system and realized that the Mongols were not just great warriors—they were brilliant administrators as well.

As months turned into years, Marco gained the trust of Kublai Khan. The Great Khan was so impressed with his intelligence and ability to learn that he gave him important missions, sending him to explore different regions of the empire and report back on what he saw. Marco traveled to the far corners of China, visited ancient temples, met wise scholars, and witnessed incredible inventions that Europe had never seen before—gunpowder, compasses, and advanced engineering techniques.

Marco Polo's time at the court of Kublai Khan was one of the most extraordinary experiences of his life. He had entered as a young traveler from a distant land, but he left as a trusted advisor and observer of one of the greatest empires in history. His journey had only just begun, but the lessons he learned at Kublai Khan's court would stay with him forever, shaping the stories he would one day bring back to the Western world.

Chapter 8: A Friendship with the Great Khan

Marco Polo's time at the court of Kublai Khan was not just about witnessing the wonders of the Mongol Empire; it was about forming a deep and lasting bond with one of the most powerful rulers in history. At first, Marco had been nothing more than a curious traveler, a guest in the Great Khan's court, but as time passed, something remarkable happened—Kublai Khan saw something special in Marco. He wasn't just another merchant or explorer passing through; he was intelligent, observant, and eager to learn. Slowly, Marco became more than just a visitor—he became a trusted member of the Khan's court, a friend to the ruler of the largest empire in the world.

Kublai Khan, the grandson of Genghis Khan, was no ordinary emperor. Unlike some rulers who cared only for conquest and power, Kublai Khan was deeply interested in knowledge, culture, and the different peoples of the world. He surrounded himself with the wisest scholars, the most skilled artisans, and the most talented diplomats. He ruled over a vast empire stretching from China to Persia, from Russia to India, and he wanted to understand all the lands and cultures under his control. Marco Polo, with his sharp mind and unique perspective as a European, fascinated him. The Great Khan asked Marco countless questions about the Western world—its rulers, its armies, its trade, and its customs. No European had ever described these things to him in such detail, and he was eager to learn more.

The more Marco spoke, the more Kublai Khan listened. Marco described the grand cities of Europe, the towering cathedrals of Italy, and the bustling trade ports of Venice. He explained how kings and queens ruled, how merchants conducted business, and how people lived in the lands far beyond the Mongol Empire. Kublai Khan, in turn, shared the wisdom of the East with Marco, teaching him about the traditions of China, the philosophies of Confucius, and the complex system of government that kept his vast empire running smoothly. Their conversations went on for hours, sometimes even late into the night. It was a meeting of two worlds—East and West—coming together in the most unexpected of friendships.

Over time, Marco became one of the Great Khan's most trusted men. He was given luxurious clothes made of the finest silk, feasted on the most delicious foods, and treated with great honor. But more importantly, he was given responsibilities. Kublai Khan did not just see Marco as a visitor; he saw him as someone useful, someone who could help him rule his empire. He began to send Marco on important missions, making him a kind of ambassador who traveled across the empire to observe, learn, and report back to the Khan.

Marco's travels took him to distant provinces, where he saw things that no European had ever witnessed before. He visited the great cities of China, filled with towering pagodas, bustling markets, and canals filled with boats. He marveled at the engineering of Chinese bridges, the brilliance of paper money, and the efficiency of the Mongol postal system, where riders could travel thousands of miles in just days to deliver messages. Everywhere he went, he reported back to Kublai Khan, describing what he had seen and what could be improved. The Great Khan valued Marco's insights and used them to strengthen his empire.

As the years passed, Marco and Kublai Khan grew closer. Despite their differences—one was a Venetian merchant, the other a Mongol emperor—they shared a deep mutual respect. Kublai Khan admired Marco's intelligence, honesty, and loyalty, while Marco admired Kublai Khan's wisdom, curiosity, and sense of justice. They laughed together, discussed great ideas, and even played games of strategy, where Kublai Khan tested Marco's mind against his own. In a world where emperors and rulers often saw foreigners as mere outsiders, Kublai Khan saw Marco as a friend.

Marco also learned the Mongol way of life. He rode swift Mongol horses across the vast plains, dined in grand feasts where roasted meats and exotic dishes were served, and watched the Great Khan's warriors demonstrate their unmatched skills in archery and combat. He saw how the Mongols treated their allies with respect but crushed their enemies without mercy. He realized that Kublai Khan's empire was built not just on conquest but on intelligence, strategy, and the ability to govern many different peoples.

Kublai Khan, in turn, treated Marco almost like an adopted son. He rewarded him with treasures, honored him before his court, and even allowed him to sit in on important meetings with governors, generals, and advisors. Marco was no longer just an observer; he had become part of the Mongol world. His time in the Great Khan's service lasted for years, longer than he had ever imagined. He had arrived in the Mongol court as a young man, and now he had grown into a seasoned traveler, a man who had seen more of the world than most could ever dream of.

But despite his incredible life in the Mongol Empire, Marco Polo never forgot where he came from. He often thought of Venice, of the canals and markets he had left behind. He missed his homeland, his people, and the familiar sights and sounds of Europe. Still, he was torn—how could he leave behind the Great Khan, the man who had shown him such kindness and trust? Kublai Khan, too, did not want Marco to leave. He valued his friend and did not wish to say goodbye.

However, as time passed, Marco knew that his journey had to continue. He and his family longed to return home, to see Venice again after so many years away. But leaving was not so simple. The Mongol Empire was vast, and the road back to Europe was filled with dangers. Moreover, Kublai Khan, now an aging ruler, was reluctant to let them go. He had grown fond of Marco and did not want to lose such a valuable companion.

But fate provided an opportunity. A Mongol princess was to be married to a Persian prince, and she needed to be escorted safely to her new home. The journey would take her across the sea, through lands that Marco had never seen before. It was a dangerous mission, but it provided Marco with a way to leave the Mongol Empire with honor. Kublai Khan, though saddened, agreed to let him go, giving him gifts, letters for the rulers of Europe, and a final farewell.

As Marco Polo set sail, he looked back at the empire he had called home for so many years. He had arrived as a young man, full of wonder and curiosity, and now he was leaving as a world traveler, forever changed by his experiences. He knew that the stories of his time with the Great Khan would amaze those back in Europe, but he also knew that nothing could ever truly capture what it was like to stand in the court of the most powerful ruler in the world.

The friendship between Marco Polo and Kublai Khan was one of history's most remarkable bonds—a connection between two very different worlds, forged through respect, trust, and a shared love of knowledge. Even after he returned home, Marco would always remember the Great Khan, the man who had welcomed him into his empire and changed his life forever.

Chapter 9: Exploring the Riches of China

When Marco Polo arrived in China, he could hardly believe his eyes. The land before him was unlike anything he had ever seen in Venice or on his long journey across the Silk Road. China, or Cathay as it was called by Europeans at the time, was a land of incredible wealth, innovation, and beauty. It was home to vast cities, towering palaces, bustling markets, and inventions that seemed almost magical. Marco had traveled thousands of miles to reach this land, and now that he was here, he was determined to explore its wonders and bring back stories that would amaze the people of Europe.

One of the first things that astonished Marco was the sheer size and splendor of China's cities. In Venice, his home, the streets were narrow, and the buildings, though grand, were nowhere near as enormous as what he found in China. The capital city, Khanbaliq—known today as Beijing—was a marvel beyond imagination. It was perfectly planned, with wide streets, grand palaces, and a city wall so massive that soldiers could ride horses along the top. The city had bustling markets filled with merchants selling silk, spices, porcelain, and precious stones. Marco had never seen such an abundance of goods in one place. The Chinese seemed to have mastered the art of trade and craftsmanship, and their wealth was unmatched.

As he wandered through the streets of Khanbaliq, Marco noticed something that seemed impossible: people were using paper money instead of gold and silver coins. In Europe, money was made of metal, but here in China, the government printed paper money with official seals. This system made trade much easier, as merchants did not have to carry heavy bags of coins. Marco was fascinated by this invention and knew that the people of Europe would be shocked to learn that money could be made of something as simple as paper.

Another wonder that amazed Marco was the intricate system of canals and waterways that connected China's cities. Unlike Europe, where most goods had to be carried on rough roads by horses and carts, China had an advanced transportation network built on rivers and canals. The Grand Canal, the longest artificial river in the world, stretched for hundreds of miles, allowing goods to be transported quickly and efficiently. Along these waterways, Marco saw large cargo boats carrying rice, silk, spices, and even exotic animals. The organization of China's trade system impressed him so much that he wrote about it in great detail, knowing that Europeans would have trouble believing that such a well-planned system existed.

Perhaps one of the most luxurious things Marco encountered in China was silk. He had heard of this precious fabric before, as it was one of the most prized goods traded on the Silk Road, but here, in the heart of China, he saw silk in ways he had never imagined. The people of China wore elegant robes made of the finest silk, decorated with golden threads and vibrant colors. The Great Khan himself was dressed in robes so magnificent that they shimmered in the sunlight. Marco visited silk workshops where skilled artisans carefully spun and wove the delicate threads, creating garments fit for emperors. The Chinese had been making silk for thousands of years, and their skill was unmatched anywhere in the world. Marco knew that if he could bring even a small piece of this silk back to Venice, it would be worth a fortune.

Beyond silk, another thing that fascinated Marco was the production of fine porcelain. In Europe, most dishes and cups were made of wood, metal, or rough clay, but in China, Marco saw delicate porcelain bowls and plates that were so thin they were almost transparent. The Chinese artisans had mastered the art of making porcelain, creating beautiful blue-and-white designs that looked like paintings. These porcelain pieces were traded all over the world, and even rulers from faraway lands sought to own them. Marco knew that such craftsmanship would be highly valued in Europe, and he made careful notes about how the Chinese produced these treasures.

One of the greatest wonders Marco saw in China was the imperial palace of Kublai Khan. This grand palace, located in the summer capital of Shangdu, was so vast that it seemed like a city of its own. The walls were covered in gold, the floors were made of precious stones, and the gardens stretched as far as the eye could see. Inside the palace, Marco saw fountains that sprayed scented water, rooms filled with priceless treasures, and feasts that could feed thousands of people at once. The Khan's banquet hall alone was so enormous that it could hold 6,000 guests, and every meal was an event of its own. Servants carried in platters of roasted meats, rice, fruits, and pastries, while musicians played beautiful melodies. Marco was astonished by the sheer wealth and luxury of the Khan's court.

Another thing that amazed Marco was the Chinese people's advanced knowledge in science, medicine, and technology. Unlike in Europe, where doctors relied on simple herbal remedies, Chinese physicians used acupuncture, a technique where thin needles were placed at specific points on the body to relieve pain and cure illnesses. They also had a deep understanding of the human body and used natural ingredients to create powerful medicines. Marco saw hospitals where patients were treated with great care, something that was rare in Europe at the time. He wrote about these medical advancements in great detail, hoping that the knowledge might one day help people in his homeland.

China's technological inventions also left Marco in awe. One of the most incredible things he witnessed was the use of gunpowder. In Europe, battles were fought with swords, bows, and catapults, but in China, Marco saw soldiers using explosive weapons. The Chinese had discovered how to mix certain minerals to create a powerful substance that could be used for fireworks, bombs, and even early forms of guns. Marco knew that this discovery would change warfare forever, and he was certain that if the secret of gunpowder reached Europe, it would give armies an entirely new way to fight.

Even everyday life in China seemed advanced compared to Europe. The cities were cleaner, the roads were well maintained, and the people were highly organized. Marco was particularly impressed by the Mongol postal system, which allowed messages to travel across the empire at incredible speed. The system was so efficient that a letter could be delivered over a thousand miles in just a few days. Riders on horseback would travel from station to station, switching to fresh horses along the way so that they never had to stop for long. This allowed the Great Khan to send orders and receive news from the farthest corners of his empire in record time.

The food in China was also unlike anything Marco had ever tasted. The Chinese had mastered the art of cooking, using spices and sauces that created flavors he had never encountered before. Noodles, dumplings, and rice dishes were common, and Marco even tried an unusual dish called "ice cream," which was cold, sweet, and delicious. He marveled at the use of tea, which people drank daily as a refreshing and healthy beverage. The way the Chinese prepared and enjoyed their food fascinated Marco, and he made sure to describe their meals in detail in his writings.

As Marco traveled deeper into China, he discovered even more wonders—temples filled with golden statues, mountains covered in mist, and cities where thousands of people lived in harmony. Everywhere he went, he was welcomed with hospitality and kindness, and he quickly learned to appreciate the wisdom and traditions of the Chinese people. He realized that Europe had much to learn from China, and he wished he could bring back not only the treasures he had seen but also the knowledge that had made this empire so great.

After spending years exploring the riches of China, Marco Polo knew that his journey had changed him forever. He had seen sights that no European had ever seen, and he had learned things that few in the West could even imagine. But he also knew that one day, he would have to leave this incredible land and return home. Even as he prepared for the long journey back, he carried with him the memories of China's wonders, knowing that he would one day share the incredible stories of this land with the rest of the world.

Chapter 10: The Secrets of Paper Money

When Marco Polo arrived in China, he discovered something that seemed almost magical—people were using paper as money instead of heavy gold and silver coins. To a traveler from Europe, where all currency was made of metal, this was one of the most astonishing things he had ever seen. In Venice and other parts of Europe, merchants carried bags of gold, silver, or copper coins to buy and sell goods. These coins were valuable because they were made of precious metals, and people trusted them. But in China, the Great Khan had introduced a system that was far more advanced—paper money.

At first, Marco could not believe that a simple piece of paper could hold any value. How could something so light and fragile be worth anything? If someone handed him a piece of paper in Venice and called it money, he would have laughed. But in China, this paper money was widely accepted, and people used it to buy goods, pay taxes, and trade in markets just as easily as they used coins. Marco quickly realized that this was not just an experiment—it was an organized and efficient system that had transformed the way people did business.

The Chinese had been using paper money for over a hundred years by the time Marco Polo arrived. The idea had started during the Tang Dynasty but was perfected under the rule of Kublai Khan, the Mongol emperor who ruled over China. The government controlled the production of paper money, ensuring that it was official and could not be easily copied. Each bill was printed with special marks and seals to prevent forgery. The money was made from a type of mulberry bark, which was strong and long-lasting. These notes came in different values, just like coins, so people could use them for small or large purchases.

Marco was amazed when he visited the imperial mint, the place where paper money was created. He saw workers carefully preparing sheets of paper, cutting them into rectangular shapes, and stamping them with official seals. Each note was signed by high-ranking officials to prove that it was genuine. The money was then distributed across the empire, allowing people from distant provinces to use the same currency without needing to carry heavy bags of coins. The Great Khan had even declared that refusing to accept paper money was a crime, ensuring that everyone in the empire trusted it.

One of the most surprising things about paper money was that it made trade much easier. In Europe, merchants who traveled long distances had to carry sacks of gold or silver, which were heavy and dangerous to transport. Thieves often targeted travelers carrying valuable coins, and there was always the risk of losing money along the way. But in China, traders could carry lightweight paper money instead, making long-distance trade safer and more convenient. This system allowed the economy to flourish, as people could buy and sell goods more freely without worrying about carrying large amounts of metal.

Marco also noticed that the Chinese had developed a banking system that worked alongside paper money. Instead of keeping all their wealth in physical coins, merchants and officials could store their money in government treasuries and receive paper notes in return. If they needed to withdraw their wealth, they could exchange the paper for gold or silver. This idea was revolutionary to Marco, as nothing like it existed in Europe at the time. In Venice, wealth was measured by the amount of gold and silver one owned, but in China, people understood that money could represent value without being made of precious metal.

Another incredible thing about China's paper money was that it allowed the government to have better control over the economy. Since the Great Khan could print money as needed, he could ensure that there was always enough currency in circulation to support trade and commerce. However, this also meant that if too much paper money was printed, it could lose its value. The Chinese had to carefully balance the supply of money to keep prices stable and prevent inflation. Marco saw how skillfully the government managed this system, and he was impressed by the level of organization and intelligence behind it.

The introduction of paper money also changed the way taxes were collected. Instead of demanding payments in heavy coins, the government accepted paper money, making it easier for people to pay what they owed. This made tax collection more efficient and allowed the empire to function smoothly. The Great Khan used the money to fund massive construction projects, including roads, canals, and palaces. He also used it to pay soldiers, ensuring that his vast empire remained well-defended.

As Marco traveled through China, he realized that paper money had many advantages over metal coins. It was lightweight, easy to carry, and could be produced in large amounts to support the economy. However, he also saw that it required trust. The people had to believe that the government-backed money had real value, even though it was just paper. Because Kublai Khan was a powerful and respected ruler, the people had confidence in his system, and it worked perfectly.

Marco Polo knew that if he told the people of Venice about paper money, they would think he was making it up. To Europeans, money had always been something tangible, something they could touch and feel in the form of gold or silver. The idea of using printed paper to buy goods and services seemed completely unbelievable. But Marco had seen it with his own eyes, and he wrote detailed accounts of how the system worked, hoping that one day, Europe might adopt a similar method.

Indeed, many centuries later, the idea of paper money spread to the rest of the world. Today, almost every country uses paper currency in some form, and it is now an essential part of global trade. Marco Polo's discovery of this incredible system was one of the most important things he brought back from China, showing Europe that there were new and better ways to manage money and trade. Though it took many years for paper money to become common outside of China, Marco's descriptions played a key role in introducing this revolutionary concept to the Western world.

In the end, Marco Polo's journey through China was filled with astonishing discoveries, but few were as impactful as his encounter with paper money. It was a system far ahead of its time, proving that the Chinese had developed an advanced economy long before Europe. Marco returned to Venice with tales of this strange but brilliant invention, and though many people doubted his stories at first, history would prove that he had witnessed one of the greatest financial innovations of all time.

Chapter 11: Adventures in the Forbidden City

When Marco Polo arrived at the heart of Kublai Khan's empire, he found himself standing before one of the most extraordinary places he had ever seen—the Forbidden City. This was not just a palace but an enormous complex of buildings, courtyards, and gardens, all designed to house the Great Khan, his family, and the most important officials of the Mongol Empire. Unlike anything Marco had ever encountered in Europe, the Forbidden City was a place of mystery, power, and unimaginable wealth. Every step he took inside its vast walls led him to new and astonishing sights, and every moment spent there was like stepping into a world that most outsiders would never get to see.

The Forbidden City was located in the capital of the empire, known as Khanbaliq, or what is today Beijing. It was called "forbidden" because ordinary people were not allowed inside. Only the emperor, his advisors, trusted servants, and honored guests could enter. Marco Polo was one of the rare foreigners permitted to walk through its gates, and this was a sign of just how much Kublai Khan trusted him. As he stepped through the grand entrance, he was immediately struck by the immense size of the complex. It stretched far beyond what the eye could see, with enormous golden-roofed halls, intricate temples, and lush gardens filled with exotic plants and animals.

One of the first things Marco noticed was the dazzling beauty of the buildings. The walls were decorated with bright colors, detailed carvings, and golden dragons that shimmered in the sunlight. Massive red pillars held up the towering roofs, and the walkways were paved with large, smooth stones. The halls of the Forbidden City were unlike anything in Europe—while European castles were often cold, dark, and made of stone, these palaces were designed to be grand yet comfortable, with airy rooms, large windows, and silk curtains that fluttered in the breeze. Every room was filled with finely crafted furniture, delicate porcelain vases, and intricate tapestries woven with silk and gold threads.

One of the most fascinating places in the Forbidden City was the throne room, where Kublai Khan held his meetings with officials, military leaders, and foreign guests. This massive hall was lined with golden statues, glowing lanterns, and walls covered in beautiful paintings. At the far end of the room sat the Great Khan himself, on a raised platform, his throne carved from rare and precious materials. The moment Marco Polo first saw him sitting there, he understood why people from all over Asia respected and feared this man. Dressed in the finest silks, wearing a golden crown, and surrounded by guards and servants, Kublai Khan looked every bit like the ruler of the most powerful empire in the world.

One of the most remarkable things Marco discovered in the Forbidden City was the way Kublai Khan ran his empire. Unlike European kings, who often ruled with absolute power and rarely listened to their subjects, the Great Khan believed in surrounding himself with intelligent advisors from different parts of the world. In the grand halls of the Forbidden City, he held court with scholars, merchants, generals, and foreign ambassadors. Marco witnessed debates about law, trade, and science, and he was amazed by the advanced knowledge of the Chinese and Mongol officials. The Great Khan encouraged learning, and he invited people from all cultures to share their ideas. He even employed scientists, mathematicians, and astrologers to help him make important decisions.

The Forbidden City was not just a place of politics and power—it was also a center of entertainment, culture, and luxury. Marco Polo was invited to lavish banquets where hundreds of guests gathered to feast on an incredible variety of dishes. The meals in the Forbidden City were nothing like the simple bread and meat Marco was used to in Venice. Instead, tables were filled with roasted meats, exotic fruits, steamed dumplings, and richly spiced dishes. There were even chefs who specialized in making dishes that only the Khan and his family could eat. The guests drank tea, a drink Marco had never tasted before, and some even sipped a special fermented milk called kumis, which was popular among the Mongols.

Entertainment in the Forbidden City was unlike anything Marco had ever seen. There were performers who could balance on tightropes, acrobats who flipped through the air, and dancers who moved gracefully to the sound of musical instruments Marco had never heard before. Musicians played flutes, drums, and stringed instruments that created melodies so different from the ones in Europe. Storytellers and poets recited tales of legendary heroes and past emperors, and magicians performed tricks that seemed impossible. The Khan was a man who loved to be entertained, and he spared no expense in making sure that his court was filled with excitement.

One of the most extraordinary sights in the Forbidden City was the Great Khan's private garden. Marco Polo had seen gardens before, but nothing like this. This was not just a place with a few trees and flowers—it was a masterpiece of design, created to bring together nature and beauty in perfect harmony. There were ponds filled with colorful fish, stone bridges arching over streams, and pavilions where the Khan could sit and enjoy the peaceful surroundings. Rare and exotic plants from different parts of the empire were carefully tended by skilled gardeners. Some trees bore fruits that Marco had never seen before, and flowers bloomed in colors he had never imagined.

Perhaps the most astonishing part of Marco's adventures in the Forbidden City was the Great Khan's vast collection of treasures. Kublai Khan was the ruler of the wealthiest empire in the world, and he had access to riches that seemed endless. There were rooms filled with gold, silver, and jewels, stacks of the finest silk from China, and rare spices from distant lands. The Forbidden City also contained some of the most advanced inventions Marco had ever seen, including complex water clocks, finely crafted weapons, and strange devices that seemed almost magical. Marco knew that if he told the people of Venice about these things, they would find it hard to believe.

But the Forbidden City was not just about wealth and luxury—it was also a place of strict rules. Every person who entered had to follow specific customs and behave with great respect. The Khan's guards were always watching, making sure that no one disrespected the emperor or broke the laws of the palace. There were secret passageways and hidden rooms that only a few people knew about, and parts of the palace that even Marco was not allowed to see. The power of the Khan was absolute, and anyone who disobeyed his commands could face severe punishment.

Despite its strict rules, Marco Polo felt honored to be one of the few foreigners to walk through the Forbidden City's halls. He knew he was witnessing something that few outsiders ever would. His time in the Forbidden City changed the way he saw the world—he realized that China was far more advanced than Europe in many ways, and that there were incredible things beyond what he had ever imagined back home. When he finally left the Forbidden City to continue his journey, he carried with him memories of a place that seemed almost too magnificent to be real.

Years later, when Marco returned to Venice and told his stories, many people refused to believe him. They thought his descriptions of the Forbidden City were too grand, too magical, to be true. But history would prove that he had indeed walked through the halls of one of the most incredible places on Earth, and his tales of the Forbidden City would inspire generations of explorers, scholars, and dreamers to come.

Chapter 12: Spices and Treasures of the East

When Marco Polo traveled through the lands of the East, he encountered a world filled with riches, wonders, and incredible treasures that people in Europe could barely imagine. Among the many things that fascinated him, nothing captured his attention more than the precious spices and luxurious goods that were traded throughout Asia. The East was a land of abundance, where merchants carried rare and valuable goods across vast distances, from bustling cities to remote villages. Marco had heard stories of these treasures before he ever set foot in China, but seeing them with his own eyes was an experience beyond anything he had ever dreamed.

Spices were among the most sought-after goods in the East, and Marco quickly learned why. In Europe, food was often bland and difficult to preserve, especially in colder months. Meat would spoil quickly, and there were few ways to add exciting flavors to meals. But in the markets of the East, Marco discovered a dazzling variety of spices that could transform ordinary food into something extraordinary. There was cinnamon, with its sweet and woody aroma; cloves, which had a strong and almost fiery taste; and nutmeg, a rare spice that was worth more than gold in some places. Marco also encountered ginger, which was both spicy and slightly sweet, and star anise, with its unusual shape and licorice-like flavor.

The most valuable spice of all was black pepper. In Europe, it was known as "black gold" because it was so expensive and rare. But in the East, Marco saw baskets filled with peppercorns, traded like common goods in the bustling markets. Merchants from India and the Spice Islands brought loads of pepper to sell, and Chinese traders used it to season their food in ways Marco had never seen before. It amazed him to learn that in some parts of the East, pepper was not just a luxury—it was a necessity, used in medicine, perfumes, and even religious ceremonies.

But spices were only a small part of the incredible treasures Marco found on his journey. Silk was another prized good, and China was famous for producing the finest silk in the world. Marco had heard stories about silk in Venice, but when he touched the smooth, shimmering fabric for the first time, he understood why it was so valuable. Chinese silk was soft, lightweight, and incredibly strong. The patterns woven into the cloth were so detailed and colorful that they seemed almost magical. The emperors of China dressed in the finest silk robes, embroidered with gold and silver threads, and wealthy merchants across Asia paid fortunes for the best silk garments.

Silk was such an important part of trade that entire caravans carried it across the Silk Road, traveling from China to Europe and beyond. Marco learned that the secret of silk-making had been closely guarded for centuries. The Chinese were the only ones who knew how to produce it, using tiny silkworms that spun delicate threads into cocoons. These threads were then carefully unwound and woven into luxurious fabric. Any outsider who tried to steal the secret of silk-making could face serious punishment, and for many years, no one outside of China knew exactly how it was made.

Another treasure that fascinated Marco Polo was porcelain. In Europe, dishes and cups were made of clay, wood, or metal, but in China, Marco saw something far more elegant—porcelain plates, bowls, and vases that were so fine and delicate that they almost seemed transparent. The Chinese had mastered the art of making porcelain, using a special kind of clay that was fired in high-temperature kilns to create smooth, beautiful ceramics. Some pieces were painted with intricate blue designs, while others were glazed in colors that shimmered in the light. Chinese porcelain was so prized that even the most powerful kings and queens in Europe longed to own it.

Jewels and precious stones were another part of the immense wealth of the East. Marco saw traders selling sapphires, rubies, emeralds, and pearls, each more dazzling than the last. Some of these gems came from the mountains of India, while others were fished from the depths of the ocean. Pearls, in particular, were among the most valuable treasures of the East. The best ones were found deep in the waters of the Persian Gulf and along the coasts of China. These pearls were not small and dull like the ones Marco had seen in Europe—they were large, smooth, and perfectly round, glowing with a soft, silvery sheen. Wealthy noblemen and women wore pearl necklaces, and even the Great Khan himself had robes decorated with strings of pearls.

One of the most mysterious and valuable goods Marco encountered was jade. This precious green stone was highly prized in China, not just for its beauty but for its special meaning. The Chinese believed that jade symbolized wisdom, strength, and good fortune. Some pieces of jade were carved into delicate figurines of dragons and phoenixes, while others were shaped into ceremonial weapons or jewelry. Marco was amazed by how carefully jade was handled—only the finest craftsmen were allowed to carve it, and some pieces took years to complete. Jade was so valuable that it was often traded for gold, silver, or even land.

In addition to silk, porcelain, and jewels, the East was also rich in exotic goods that were completely new to Marco. He saw paper being used for writing, something that was still rare in Europe at the time. Chinese paper was smooth and lightweight, making it much easier to write on than the rough parchment used in Venice. Books made of paper were common in China, and Marco even saw entire libraries filled with scrolls of ancient knowledge. He also learned about printing, a revolutionary process that allowed books and documents to be copied quickly using carved wooden blocks. In Europe, books were copied by hand, taking months or even years to produce, so the idea of printing seemed like something out of a dream.

One of the strangest and most fascinating things Marco saw in the markets of the East was paper money. In Venice, all trade was done with coins made of gold, silver, or copper, but in China, merchants used pieces of paper stamped with official seals as money. At first, Marco could not believe that people would accept paper in exchange for valuable goods, but he soon learned that the system worked because of the trust people had in the emperor. The Great Khan's government controlled the production of paper money, and everyone knew that they could exchange it for gold or other goods if needed. This made trade much easier because merchants did not have to carry heavy bags of coins wherever they went.

As Marco Polo traveled through the cities and markets of the East, he was overwhelmed by the incredible variety of goods available. He saw spices and rare herbs being traded alongside silk and gold. He walked through marketplaces where merchants sold ivory from Africa, perfumes from Arabia, and carpets from Persia. He even witnessed strange and wonderful inventions that had not yet reached Europe, such as mechanical clocks, gunpowder, and compasses that helped sailors navigate the seas. Every day brought a new discovery, and every market was filled with wonders that made Marco realize just how vast and rich the world truly was.

By the time Marco Polo finally returned to Venice, he carried with him stories of the incredible treasures of the East. He described the dazzling markets of China, the rare spices of India, and the silk caravans that crossed the deserts. Many people in Venice did not believe his tales—they thought he was exaggerating or making things up. But in the years that followed, as trade between East and West grew, the world began to see that Marco Polo had spoken the truth. His journey had opened the eyes of Europe to the wealth and wonders of the East, inspiring future explorers to follow in his footsteps and seek out the treasures of distant lands.

Chapter 13: A Journey to the Land of Gold

Marco Polo had already seen incredible wonders on his travels—towering mountains, vast deserts, bustling cities, and rich marketplaces filled with treasures beyond imagination. But there was one place that sparked even more curiosity in his heart—a land so wealthy, so filled with gold, that people in the East spoke of it with awe and admiration. This was the fabled kingdom of gold, a place that Marco longed to see with his own eyes. He had heard stories about a distant land where golden temples shimmered under the sun, where the rulers possessed fortunes beyond belief, and where trade flourished like nowhere else. The tales of this place had spread far and wide, and Marco, ever the fearless explorer, was determined to uncover the truth behind the legend.

As he traveled through the vast empire of Kublai Khan, he heard more and more whispers about this golden land. Some said it lay far to the south, beyond great rivers and towering mountains. Others claimed it was hidden deep within dense jungles, guarded by fierce warriors and surrounded by treacherous waters. The Great Khan himself was eager to expand his influence over this wealthy land, and when Marco Polo offered to travel there as an envoy, the mighty ruler agreed. Thus, Marco set off on yet another daring adventure, sailing across vast seas and traversing unfamiliar lands in search of the fabled kingdom of gold.

His journey began in the great port cities of China, where ships from all over the world came to trade silk, spices, and precious gems. The harbors bustled with activity—sailors shouted orders as they loaded and unloaded cargo, merchants haggled over the prices of rare goods, and curious travelers from distant lands shared stories of their homelands. Marco boarded a grand ship, its sails billowing in the wind as it set off toward the unknown. The sea voyage was long and dangerous, with powerful storms threatening to capsize the ship and fierce waves crashing against its wooden hull. But Marco was not afraid—he had survived deserts, mountains, and freezing winters, and he was determined to complete this journey.

After weeks at sea, Marco and his companions finally spotted land on the horizon. As they approached the shore, they saw lush forests, towering palm trees, and golden beaches stretching as far as the eye could see. They had arrived in a new and mysterious land, one unlike anything Marco had seen before. The air was thick with the scent of exotic flowers and spices, and the sounds of unfamiliar birds and animals filled the jungle. Marco and his group stepped onto the sandy shores, eager to explore the wonders that lay ahead.

As they ventured further inland, they encountered villages where the people dressed in brightly colored garments woven from fine fabrics. They wore intricate jewelry made of gold, silver, and rare gemstones, and their homes were decorated with beautiful carvings and golden ornaments. The people welcomed Marco and his companions with curiosity, offering them exotic fruits, fragrant spices, and delicious foods unlike anything they had ever tasted. Marco marveled at the abundance of wealth in this land—gold was not just a rare treasure here, but something that seemed to be everywhere. The rulers of this kingdom were said to possess entire palaces made of gold, and their temples shone like the sun itself.

Marco learned that gold was not just a sign of wealth in this land—it held deep cultural and religious significance. The people believed that gold was a gift from the heavens, a metal so pure that it could bring blessings and good fortune. The great temples were adorned with golden statues of deities, their faces glowing in the candlelight, and the royal palaces gleamed with golden rooftops and intricately decorated walls. Even the everyday objects used by the wealthy—cups, plates, and jewelry—were made of solid gold. Marco had never seen such a place before, and he understood why the tales of this golden kingdom had spread across the world.

As he traveled through the land, Marco visited bustling markets where merchants traded not only gold but also rare spices, pearls, and precious stones. He saw baskets overflowing with cinnamon, saffron, and nutmeg, and he learned that these spices were as valuable as gold in distant lands. The people of this kingdom were skilled traders, exchanging their riches for silk, ivory, and rare goods from faraway places. Marco watched as traders measured gold dust with delicate scales, ensuring that each transaction was fair and honest. He was fascinated by how gold was woven into every part of life in this land—used not just for trade, but for beauty, worship, and even medicine.

But Marco's journey was not without danger. The golden kingdom was a place of wealth, and with great riches came great risks. Pirates roamed the seas, hoping to capture ships laden with treasures, and bandits lurked in the dense jungles, waiting to ambush travelers carrying gold and precious gems. The rulers of this land had built mighty fortresses to protect their wealth, with high walls, watchtowers, and guards armed with powerful weapons. Marco learned that some of these warriors had swords and armor made with gold, symbols of their strength and loyalty to their king.

Despite the dangers, Marco continued his exploration, meeting rulers, merchants, and travelers who had come to this land seeking fortune. He documented everything he saw, describing the grand palaces, the golden temples, and the customs of the people. He wrote about the vast mines where gold was carefully extracted from deep within the earth, and he detailed the complex methods used to shape the precious metal into intricate designs. Every discovery fascinated him, and he knew that when he returned to Venice, the tales of this golden land would astound everyone who heard them.

After spending many months in the golden kingdom, Marco finally prepared to leave. He had gathered incredible knowledge, seen riches beyond his wildest dreams, and experienced a way of life completely different from his own. As he boarded his ship to return to the court of Kublai Khan, he carried with him not only gold and treasures but also memories of an adventure that would forever change his view of the world.

When Marco Polo finally returned to Venice years later, he shared the tales of his journey with anyone who would listen. Many people doubted his stories—how could a land so rich in gold truly exist? But as time passed and more explorers ventured eastward, they confirmed that Marco's tales were not just fantasies. He had indeed traveled to a land of gold, a place of wealth, beauty, and wonder. His journey inspired future adventurers to seek out new lands, new riches, and new connections between East and West.

Marco Polo's journey to the land of gold was not just about discovering wealth—it was about uncovering the incredible diversity of the world. He had seen how different cultures valued gold, how trade connected distant lands, and how wealth could shape a civilization. His adventure proved that the world was far larger and more fascinating than most people in Europe had ever imagined. And though he had traveled thousands of miles, braved countless dangers, and witnessed unimaginable riches, he knew that the greatest treasure of all was the knowledge he had gained along the way.

Chapter 14: Facing Dangers on the Road

Marco Polo had already traveled thousands of miles, crossing vast deserts, towering mountains, and roaring rivers. But his journey was far from easy. Every step of the way, he faced dangers that tested his courage, endurance, and intelligence. Traveling across unknown lands was not just about discovering new places—it was about surviving the many threats that lurked along the road. The farther Marco and his companions traveled, the more they realized that the road ahead was filled with obstacles, both from nature and from the people they encountered.

One of the greatest dangers Marco faced was the unpredictable and often brutal forces of nature. As he journeyed across the mighty Gobi Desert, he quickly learned that this was one of the most treacherous places in the world. The desert stretched endlessly in every direction, with nothing but sand dunes, dry riverbeds, and rocky plains. The sun blazed mercilessly during the day, turning the ground beneath them into scorching fire, while the nights became so cold that it felt as if they had entered an icy wasteland. There was little water to be found, and the small oases scattered throughout the desert were few and far between. If they missed one, they could be doomed.

The desert held another terrifying danger—sandstorms. These powerful storms could appear out of nowhere, swirling up enormous clouds of dust and sand that blotted out the sun. The wind howled like a wild beast, tearing through their camp and making it nearly impossible to see. Marco and his fellow travelers had to cover their faces with cloth to keep from choking on the thick sand. Sometimes, the storms were so strong that they buried entire caravans under mountains of sand, never to be found again. There were also eerie stories of desert spirits that lured travelers off their path, leading them deeper into the wilderness where they would never be seen again. Though Marco did not believe in spirits, he understood that getting lost in the desert was a real and deadly threat.

But deserts were not the only natural obstacles. As Marco traveled through the towering mountains of Central Asia, he encountered freezing temperatures, avalanches, and deadly cliffs. The snow-covered peaks of the Pamir Mountains were among the highest in the world, and climbing them was a dangerous challenge. The thin air at such high altitudes made it difficult to breathe, and every step felt like a battle against exhaustion. Slippery ice and loose rocks made the journey even riskier, and one wrong step could send a traveler tumbling down into a deep, icy gorge. Marco and his group had to rely on experienced guides who knew the safest paths, but even then, the mountains were unforgiving.

Wild animals also posed a constant threat. In the dense forests and grasslands, Marco encountered fearsome creatures he had never seen before. Packs of wolves followed their caravan at night, their glowing eyes watching from the darkness, waiting for an opportunity to strike. In some regions, massive bears roamed the mountains, strong enough to tear apart a man with a single swipe of their claws. Venomous snakes slithered silently through the underbrush, and deadly scorpions hid under rocks, ready to sting anyone who disturbed them. Marco had to be constantly alert, knowing that even a single careless moment could cost him his life.

However, nature was not the only danger on the road. The human threats were just as terrifying. Bandits and thieves roamed the trade routes, hiding in mountain passes, forests, and remote desert trails, waiting to ambush unsuspecting travelers. Caravans like Marco's carried valuable goods—silk, spices, gold, and jewels—making them a perfect target. Some bandits were ruthless, attacking travelers with swords and bows, stealing everything they could, and sometimes even leaving no survivors. Others were more cunning, disguising themselves as friendly traders or lost travelers to gain trust before betraying their victims.

Marco quickly learned that traveling safely meant being prepared for anything. He and his companions always traveled in large groups, knowing that there was strength in numbers. They hired armed guards to protect them, and they kept watch at night to make sure no one tried to sneak into their camp. Whenever they entered a dangerous region, they moved quickly and avoided drawing attention to themselves. Sometimes, they even paid bribes to local warlords or tribal leaders to ensure safe passage.

In some areas, war and political conflicts made travel even more dangerous. Rival kingdoms fought over land and trade routes, and Marco sometimes found himself caught in the middle of these struggles. Soldiers patrolled the roads, questioning travelers and demanding taxes or tolls. Some rulers were suspicious of foreigners, and getting past their borders required careful negotiation. Marco's ability to communicate in multiple languages and his skills as a diplomat helped him avoid trouble in many situations, but there were times when he had to rely on the protection of the Great Khan's name to pass through safely.

Disease was another invisible but deadly danger. The long journey exposed Marco and his companions to many different climates, foods, and people, increasing their risk of sickness. In the crowded marketplaces and caravanserais where travelers gathered, illnesses spread quickly. Without modern medicine, even a simple infection could turn deadly. Marco saw people suffering from fevers, coughing uncontrollably, or covered in strange rashes. He had to be extremely careful with what he ate and drank, making sure that his food was well-cooked and his water was clean. Sometimes, they had to travel for days without proper food or rest, which made them even more vulnerable to sickness.

Despite all these dangers, Marco never gave up. He faced each challenge with determination, learning from every obstacle he encountered. He developed survival skills, relied on the knowledge of local guides, and stayed alert at all times. Every hardship made him stronger and more prepared for the journey ahead. He knew that the road was not just about reaching a destination—it was about the experiences, the lessons, and the incredible stories that he would one day share with the world.

By the time he finally returned to Venice after more than two decades of travel, Marco Polo had faced nearly every danger imaginable. He had conquered deserts, climbed mountains, survived attacks, and outwitted enemies. His journey proved that with courage, intelligence, and perseverance, even the most perilous road could be traveled. His stories of adventure, danger, and survival would inspire generations of explorers, proving that the world was a vast and wondrous place, waiting for those brave enough to venture into the unknown.

Chapter 15: The Long Voyage Back Home

After spending many years in the grand court of Kublai Khan, Marco Polo had seen wonders beyond his wildest dreams. He had traveled through vast deserts, crossed towering mountains, marveled at glittering palaces, and witnessed the incredible wealth of China. He had served as an emissary for the Great Khan, exploring lands that no European had ever seen before. But as time passed, he began to long for his homeland. Venice, the city of his birth, seemed like a distant memory. He wondered what had changed, if his family was still there, and if he would ever see the familiar canals and stone bridges of his home again. Yet, leaving the service of the most powerful ruler in the world was not a simple task. Marco had earned the Khan's trust, and the ruler did not want to part with such a valuable and knowledgeable advisor.

For years, Marco and his father and uncle had asked for permission to return home, but each time, Kublai Khan refused. He had grown fond of them, especially Marco, whose keen observations and diplomatic skills had made him an important part of the royal court. The Khan relied on them for many tasks, and he was not eager to let them go. But time was moving forward, and Marco knew that if he did not leave soon, he might never see his homeland again.

The opportunity to return finally came in an unexpected way. A Mongol princess, Kokachin, was to be sent to Persia for marriage. The journey was long and dangerous, and the Great Khan needed trustworthy people to escort her. Seeing this as their only chance, Marco and his family volunteered to accompany the princess on her journey. Kublai Khan, though reluctant, finally agreed. He provided them with official travel documents, gifts, and enough supplies to ensure a safe voyage. It was a bittersweet farewell. Marco had spent so many years in the service of the Khan that China had almost felt like home. But the call of Venice was stronger than ever, and he was ready to begin the long voyage back.

Their journey home was no simple task. Unlike their trip to China, which had taken them overland across the Silk Road, this time they would travel mostly by sea. They boarded a fleet of ships, heavily loaded with supplies, valuable goods, and gifts from the Khan. The voyage took them through the treacherous waters of the South China Sea, across the vast Indian Ocean, and past many exotic lands that Marco had never seen before.

The sea was unpredictable, and the journey quickly turned perilous. Storms lashed their ships, with towering waves crashing down upon the decks. The winds howled, tearing at the sails and threatening to capsize their vessels. The sailors struggled to keep control, sometimes forced to throw cargo overboard to keep the ships from sinking. There were days when the sea was calm and the journey felt smooth, but those peaceful moments were always followed by new challenges.

Disease soon spread among the travelers. The combination of stale food, contaminated water, and cramped quarters made sickness inevitable. Many of the crew and passengers fell ill, including members of the princess's entourage. Without proper medicine, the sickness claimed many lives, and their numbers dwindled. The further they traveled, the more losses they suffered. Of the hundreds of people who had set sail at the beginning of the journey, only a small fraction would make it to the end. Marco and his family, though weary and weakened, were among the survivors.

Their route took them through the islands of what is now Indonesia, where they encountered exotic animals, lush jungles, and thriving trade ports filled with spices, pearls, and gold. Marco observed everything with great fascination, adding more details to the stories he would one day tell. They stopped in Sri Lanka, where they marveled at the towering temples and the legendary mountain believed to hold the footprint of Buddha. Every new land was a discovery, but their main goal was always to push forward toward home.

Finally, after months at sea, they reached Persia. The Mongol princess was safely delivered to her new home, but the journey was still not over for Marco and his family. From there, they traveled overland, crossing through war-torn regions and politically unstable territories. The Mongol Empire, once strong and united, was beginning to fracture, making travel even more dangerous. They had to be cautious, avoiding bandits, rival warlords, and treacherous roads.

As they moved westward, Marco felt the excitement build. They passed through lands that once seemed distant and unknown but now felt familiar. They crossed the mountains and deserts of Persia, retraced their steps through Armenia, and reached the edges of the Byzantine Empire. With every passing day, the idea of home felt more real.

When they finally reached the Mediterranean, it was as if the world had opened up before them. They secured passage on a ship heading toward Venice, and for the first time in more than twenty years, Marco saw the familiar blue waters that led to his city. The journey had been long, filled with dangers and losses, but he had made it.

When he stepped onto the docks of Venice, he found that much had changed. The city was still a thriving hub of trade and culture, but people no longer recognized him. He and his family had been gone for so long that many had assumed they were dead. Even their own relatives could hardly believe it was really them. Dressed in foreign clothing, speaking of lands that seemed more like myths than reality, Marco must have seemed like a stranger in his own home. But he had returned, carrying with him the greatest treasure of all—his stories.

Though his voyage back home had been filled with hardships, Marco knew that he had experienced something truly extraordinary. His journey had taken him farther than most could ever dream, and he had witnessed a world few Europeans had ever seen. Little did he know that his adventures were far from over. His tales would one day be written down, inspiring explorers for generations to come. The long voyage back home had not just been a return—it was the beginning of a legend.

Chapter 16: A Stranger in His Own Land

After more than two decades of traveling through distant lands, crossing vast deserts, braving stormy seas, and living in the court of the great Kublai Khan, Marco Polo finally returned to Venice. He had left as a young man, full of curiosity and wonder, and now he was returning as a seasoned traveler, with stories beyond imagination. But as he stepped onto the familiar docks of Venice, he quickly realized that something felt different. The city was still the same in many ways—its canals still glistened under the golden sun, its marketplaces bustled with merchants from around the world, and its grand palaces stood tall along the waterways. Yet, despite all these familiar sights, Marco felt strangely out of place. He had been gone for so long that Venice had changed in ways he had not expected, and worse, it seemed that Venice no longer recognized him.

The people on the streets did not turn to greet him. No one rushed forward to welcome him back. He had imagined this moment many times during his long journey home, thinking of warm embraces from old friends and family, excited shouts of recognition, and joyful reunions. But instead, he was met with puzzled looks. His clothes were not like those of the Venetians. He had dressed in fine silks from China, embroidered with patterns unseen in Italy. His manner of speaking, though still Venetian, carried traces of foreign lands, influenced by years spent among Mongols, Persians, and Chinese. His skin had been darkened by the sun of the deserts and the sea, and his eyes had seen things no one else in Venice could even imagine.

Even his own relatives struggled to believe it was really him. His family, the Polos, had been an important merchant house, but after so many years of silence, people had assumed that Marco, his father Niccolò, and his uncle Maffeo had perished on their journey. Some of their wealth and property had been divided among other family members, and their names had begun to fade from memory. When they arrived at the family home, they were not immediately recognized. Some even thought they were impostors trying to claim an inheritance that did not belong to them.

Marco's return was not met with the fanfare he had imagined, but rather with suspicion and disbelief. People asked, "Where have you been all these years?" When Marco and his father and uncle tried to explain, the Venetians found it impossible to believe. How could one man have traveled so far? How could he have met Kublai Khan, one of the most powerful rulers in the world? How could he have seen such wonders—palaces covered in gold, mountains that breathed fire, birds that could write, and cities so vast that Venice seemed tiny in comparison?

To prove that he was truly who he claimed to be, Marco and his family did something dramatic. They invited their relatives and some of Venice's wealthy merchants to a grand banquet. At first, the guests were skeptical, whispering among themselves that these travelers were nothing more than storytellers spinning wild fantasies. But then, Marco and his family did something remarkable. They brought out the fine silk robes they had worn in the East and cut them open, revealing hidden treasures sewn inside the linings—glistening rubies, sparkling emeralds, shining gold coins, and exotic pearls. The guests gasped in astonishment. No Venetian had ever seen such wealth. Suddenly, they realized that Marco had indeed traveled to the farthest reaches of the world.

Even with this proof, many still doubted his tales. They found it hard to believe that paper money could exist, that people in the East bathed every day, or that an entire army could be made up of fierce Mongol warriors who could ride for days without rest. They thought his stories were entertaining, but too fantastic to be true. Some even gave him a nickname—"Il Milione," meaning "The Man of a Million Lies." Though Marco insisted that everything he said was true, there were always those who believed he was exaggerating.

Venice itself had changed while Marco was away. Once, it had been a city he knew like the back of his hand, but now, many things were unfamiliar. New merchants had risen to power, alliances had shifted, and younger generations had taken over. Some streets looked the same, but others had new buildings he did not recognize. The city's politics had evolved, and Venice was now in a fierce rivalry with Genoa, another powerful trading city. The world had not stood still while Marco was away, and adjusting to his homeland again was not easy.

Despite the challenges, Marco was determined to settle back into Venetian life. He resumed work as a merchant, using his knowledge of the East to trade valuable goods. He shared his experiences with those who would listen, and little by little, he regained his place in society. But his adventure was not yet over. In 1298, just a few years after his return, Venice went to war with Genoa. Marco, like many other Venetian nobles, took up arms and joined the battle at sea. However, the battle did not go well for Venice, and Marco was captured by the Genoese. He was thrown into prison, locked away in a dark, stone cell, far from the riches of Kublai Khan's palace or the bustling markets of China.

But it was in this prison that Marco's greatest adventure truly began. His cellmate was a man named Rustichello da Pisa, a writer who loved grand stories. With nothing else to do, Marco began telling Rustichello about all the places he had seen. He described the beauty of the Forbidden City, the wealth of the Mongol Empire, the strange customs of faraway lands, and the dangers he had faced. Rustichello, fascinated by Marco's words, began writing everything down. Over time, these stories became a book—*The Travels of Marco Polo*—one of the most famous travel books in history.

Marco eventually gained his freedom and returned to Venice, but he never traveled as far again. He married, raised a family, and continued his work as a merchant. Though he lived the rest of his life in his homeland, he was forever marked by the years he had spent in the

East. Even on his deathbed, when people asked him if his stories were true, he is said to have replied, "I have not told half of what I saw."

Marco Polo had returned to his home, but in many ways, he remained a stranger in his own land. His mind was filled with memories of golden palaces, vast deserts, powerful emperors, and bustling cities. Though he had set foot in Venice once more, a part of him always remained in the lands he had traveled. His heart belonged not just to the canals of his childhood, but to the wide world he had explored—one that few in his homeland could ever truly understand.

Chapter 17: Sharing Tales of the East

After spending more than two decades traveling across the vast lands of Asia, living in the court of Kublai Khan, and witnessing wonders beyond imagination, Marco Polo finally returned home to Venice. But he did not return empty-handed. While he brought back silks, spices, and treasures from the East, the most valuable thing he carried with him was not gold or jewels—it was his stories. Marco had seen things that no one in Europe had ever imagined, and he was eager to share his incredible experiences. Yet, when he began telling people about his adventures, he quickly realized that many found his tales too astonishing to believe.

At first, Marco tried telling his family and friends about what he had seen in China and the Mongol Empire. He spoke of great cities filled with buildings covered in gold, rivers teeming with boats, roads so wide that ten horse-drawn carriages could travel side by side, and markets filled with exotic goods. He described Kublai Khan's magnificent palace, where walls sparkled with gold and silver, and the great hall could fit thousands of people. He spoke of towers so high they seemed to touch the sky, of bridges longer than anything built in Europe, and of entire cities lit by glowing lanterns at night. But instead of being amazed, many people laughed at him.

"How could such things exist?" they scoffed. "Surely, Marco is making up these stories!" Some even started calling him *Il Milione*, meaning "The Man of a Million Lies." They found it impossible to believe that somewhere far away, people used paper money instead of gold and silver coins, or that the Mongol Empire had an organized postal system where messages could travel faster than anywhere in Europe. They could not imagine a world where people drank hot tea instead of wine, or where houses were built with bamboo instead of stone.

But Marco did not give up. He knew what he had seen, and he was determined to share it. He told stories of the Great Wall of China, a structure so long and strong that no army could break through it. He spoke of black stones that burned like wood—coal, something almost unknown in Europe at the time. He described the Mongol warriors who could ride for days without stopping, drinking mare's milk to survive and shooting arrows with incredible accuracy even while galloping at full speed. He talked about the strange animals he had seen—giant serpents in India, enormous birds that could carry elephants into the sky, and even unicorns, which were actually rhinoceroses.

Still, people doubted him. Venice was a wealthy city, but it was small compared to the grand capitals Marco had seen. The people of Venice could not imagine a place where streets were paved with stone, where the Khan ruled over millions of people, or where markets stretched for miles selling spices, silk, pearls, and jade. They had never seen fireworks that burst into colorful lights in the sky, nor had they heard of great feasts where hundreds of different dishes were served. Marco had to work hard to convince them that the world was far bigger than they had ever imagined.

Then, something unexpected happened. In 1298, a war broke out between Venice and Genoa, another powerful trading city. Marco, like many Venetian nobles, joined the fight, sailing on one of Venice's great ships. But during the battle, he was captured by the Genoese and thrown into prison. At first, this seemed like a terrible fate—locked away in a cold, dark cell, far from the grand adventures of his past. But it was in this prison that Marco's stories would finally come to life in a way that would change history.

In his prison cell, Marco met another captive—a man named Rustichello da Pisa. Rustichello was a writer, known for creating tales of knights and heroes. As the two men sat together, Marco began telling Rustichello about his travels, filling the long days in prison with tales of the Silk Road, the Mongol Empire, and the wonders of the East. Rustichello, fascinated by these incredible stories, decided to write them down. He recorded Marco's words on parchment, creating a book that would later be known as *The Travels of Marco Polo*.

For months, Marco told Rustichello everything he could remember. He described the cities he had visited, the customs of the people he had met, the foods he had tasted, and the dangers he had faced. He spoke of the vast deserts where travelers had to follow the stars to avoid getting lost, of mountains where the air was so thin it was hard to breathe, and of islands where spices grew in abundance. He told of strange beliefs and traditions, of emperors with enormous wealth, and of inventions that did not exist in Europe, like printed books, gunpowder, and compasses used for navigation.

When the book was finished, it was unlike anything Europe had ever seen. It was not just a simple travel journal—it was an adventure filled with descriptions of lands most Europeans had never even heard of. The book spread quickly, copied by hand and passed from city to city. Some people read it with amazement, while others still doubted its truth. But whether they believed it or not, they could not ignore it. Marco's tales captured the imagination of explorers, traders, and even kings.

Over time, *The Travels of Marco Polo* became one of the most important books of the Middle Ages. It inspired merchants to seek out the riches of the East, encouraging more trade between Europe and Asia. It gave explorers new ideas about the world, leading to the great Age of Exploration. In fact, centuries later, a young sailor named Christopher Columbus read Marco Polo's book and became so fascinated by the East that he set out to find a new route to Asia—only to stumble upon the Americas instead.

Even in his later years, Marco continued to tell his stories, though there were always those who doubted him. On his deathbed, when asked if he had made up his tales, Marco is said to have replied, "I have not told half of what I saw." Whether people believed him or not, there was no doubt that his stories had changed the way Europe saw the world.

Marco Polo may have returned to Venice, but in many ways, he never truly left the lands he had explored. His heart remained with the golden palaces of Kublai Khan, the bustling markets of China, the great ships sailing across distant seas, and the vast deserts he had once crossed. Through his book, he ensured that the world would remember the wonders he had witnessed, inspiring generations of travelers to set out on their own adventures, seeking the marvels of lands unknown.

Chapter 18: The Book That Shocked Europe

When Marco Polo returned home to Venice after spending more than twenty years traveling across Asia, he carried with him something far more valuable than gold, silk, or spices—he carried knowledge. He had seen wonders that no European had ever laid eyes on. He had walked through cities larger and grander than any in Europe, met rulers more powerful than European kings, and encountered inventions that seemed like magic. But when he started telling people about his experiences, he was met with disbelief. His stories were so incredible that many refused to believe them. Some even mocked him, calling him *Il Milione*, meaning "The Man of a Million Lies."

Marco Polo's journey had taken him across the treacherous Silk Road, over towering mountains, through scorching deserts, and into the heart of the Mongol Empire, where he had become a trusted advisor to the great Kublai Khan. He had seen paper money being used instead of gold and silver, watched fireworks explode in dazzling colors in the night sky, and observed a postal system so efficient that messages could travel thousands of miles in just a few days. He had visited lands where spices grew in abundance, where people drank tea instead of wine, and where magnificent palaces gleamed with gold. But back in Venice, his tales seemed too fantastic to be real.

Then, something unexpected happened. In 1298, a war broke out between Venice and Genoa, a powerful rival city-state. Marco, like many Venetian nobles, joined the fight and set sail for battle. But in a fierce naval clash, he was captured by the Genoese and thrown into prison. For most men, this would have been a terrible fate—locked away in a dark, damp cell, far from home, with no idea when they would be freed. But for Marco Polo, this imprisonment turned out to be a stroke of luck. It was here, in a Genoese prison, that his legendary book was born.

Inside his prison cell, Marco met another captive, a man named Rustichello da Pisa. Rustichello was a writer, known for composing tales of knights and heroes. The two men quickly became friends, and Marco, with nothing else to do, began telling Rustichello about his incredible journey to the East. Night after night, Marco described his adventures—his time in the court of Kublai Khan, the bustling markets of China, the vast deserts of Persia, and the wonders of lands beyond Europe's imagination. Rustichello, fascinated by these incredible stories, decided to write them down. Using parchment and ink, he carefully recorded every detail, turning Marco's spoken words into a book that would change history.

When Marco Polo was finally released from prison in 1299, he returned to Venice, but his stories did not stay locked away. His book, known as *The Travels of Marco Polo*, quickly began spreading across Europe. At first, it was copied by hand and passed from city to city, read by merchants, scholars, and rulers alike. Some were amazed, others were skeptical, but no one could ignore it. The book described places and cultures that few in Europe even knew existed. It spoke of lands rich with silk, spices, and gold, of roads so well built that armies could march across them with ease, and of palaces more magnificent than any castle in Europe.

One of the most shocking things in the book was Marco's description of paper money. In Europe, people used heavy gold and silver coins for trade, but in China, the Mongols used lightweight paper bills, stamped with the emperor's seal, which could be exchanged for goods. To Europeans, this idea seemed impossible—how could a simple piece of paper hold any value? Many dismissed it as a fantasy, but in time, the world would come to see that Marco had described the future of money.

Marco also wrote about coal, which he called "black stones that burn like wood." In Europe, people mostly burned wood to heat their homes and cook their food, but in China, coal was used as a powerful fuel that could burn for hours. At the time, few Europeans paid attention to this discovery, but centuries later, coal would become the driving force behind the Industrial Revolution.

Another astonishing part of Marco's book was his description of the Mongol postal system. In Europe, sending a message across a country could take weeks or even months, but in the Mongol Empire, an organized network of postal stations allowed messages to travel hundreds of miles in a single day. Riders on horseback would pass messages from station to station, ensuring that important news reached the Khan quickly. This level of communication was unheard of in Europe, and many believed Marco had exaggerated the system's efficiency.

Marco also wrote about exotic animals that seemed like creatures from a fantasy story. He described giant serpents in India that could swallow a man whole, birds so large that they could carry elephants into the sky, and "unicorns" that looked nothing like the elegant, white horses from European legends—they were actually rhinoceroses! He also spoke of the panda, a black-and-white bear that no one in Europe had ever heard of before. His accounts of these animals seemed so unbelievable that many dismissed them as fairy tales.

The book also introduced Europe to the wealth of spices found in the East. In those days, spices were more valuable than gold, as they were used to preserve food, add flavor, and even create medicines. Marco described vast markets filled with cinnamon, cloves, nutmeg, and black pepper—things that were incredibly rare and expensive in Europe. His descriptions fueled the dreams of merchants who longed to find a direct route to these lands, setting the stage for future explorers like Vasco da Gama and Christopher Columbus.

One of the most shocking claims in Marco's book was the size and splendor of Chinese cities. At a time when the largest European cities had populations of maybe 50,000 people, Marco described cities in China with more than a million inhabitants, grand roads, organized markets, and stunning architecture. He wrote about Hangzhou, a city so large that it had ten marketplaces, each bigger than any market in Venice. He spoke of Beijing, the capital of the Mongol Empire, where the Khan's palace was so vast that it could hold thousands of people at once. To Europeans, who were used to small, crowded towns, these descriptions seemed beyond belief.

Many readers were fascinated, but others refused to believe Marco's tales. Some accused him of exaggeration, while others dismissed the book as pure fiction. How could there be a civilization more advanced than Europe? How could there be a ruler more powerful than the kings of France or England? How could there be ships larger than any in the Mediterranean, capable of crossing entire oceans? The book raised more questions than answers.

Despite the doubts, *The Travels of Marco Polo* became one of the most influential books of the Middle Ages. It was translated into multiple languages, copied by hand, and eventually printed when the printing press was invented. It inspired merchants to trade with the East, sparked curiosity about distant lands, and planted the seeds of the great Age of Exploration. The most famous explorer influenced by Marco Polo was Christopher Columbus, who read the book and dreamed of finding a new route to Asia. He even took a copy of *The Travels of Marco Polo* with him on his voyage in 1492, hoping to reach the lands Marco had described.

As the years passed, more and more of Marco's stories were proven true. Paper money became the standard for trade, coal fueled the modern world, and global exploration connected the East and West like never before. While many doubted Marco during his lifetime, history has since shown that his book was not just a collection of tall tales—it was a glimpse into a world that Europe had yet to discover.

Marco Polo's book did more than shock Europe; it changed the way people saw the world. It opened their eyes to new possibilities, new inventions, and new lands waiting to be explored. Though Marco himself would never sail to China again, his stories continued to travel across the globe, inspiring adventurers for centuries to come.

Chapter 19: Doubters and Believers

When Marco Polo returned to Venice after more than two decades of traveling across Asia, he was filled with excitement. He had seen things that no other European had ever seen. He had walked through golden palaces, stood before powerful emperors, traveled across vast deserts, and sailed on great rivers that stretched farther than the eye could see. He had lived in the grand court of Kublai Khan, explored the bustling markets of China, and witnessed customs, traditions, and inventions that seemed like magic. He had been to places that most people in Europe had never even heard of.

But there was just one problem—when Marco Polo told his fellow Venetians about his adventures, many of them did not believe him. Some people were amazed by his stories, eager to learn about the distant lands he had visited. Others, however, laughed at his tales, saying they were nothing but wild exaggerations. Some even called him a liar, refusing to believe that such incredible things could exist beyond the borders of Europe.

At the time, the world outside of Europe was largely unknown to the average Venetian. Most people had never traveled beyond their own city, let alone to distant lands like Persia, India, or China. To them, Venice was the center of civilization, and the idea that there were places far greater and more advanced than their own city was difficult to accept. They had never seen paper money, coal, or fireworks. They had never imagined cities with millions of people or emperors who ruled over vast empires. So, when Marco Polo spoke of these things, they thought he was either mistaken or making them up.

Some of the most unbelievable parts of Marco's stories included his descriptions of the Mongol Empire. He spoke of Kublai Khan as a ruler who controlled more land than any European king, commanding millions of people and having wealth beyond imagination. He described the Khan's palace as being so vast that it could hold thousands of people at once. He told of couriers who could deliver messages across the empire in just a few days, thanks to an advanced postal system with relay stations and fresh horses. To Europeans, who were used to slow messengers and poor roads, this sounded impossible.

Even more shocking was Marco's description of paper money. In Europe, gold and silver were the only accepted forms of currency. The idea that a piece of paper could be used to buy goods and services seemed ridiculous. How could something so light and flimsy be worth anything? Some people accused Marco of inventing such nonsense, while others laughed at the idea. But in China, paper money had been in use for many years, and Marco had seen firsthand how powerful and efficient it was.

Then there were the stories about exotic animals. Marco Polo described creatures that Europeans had never heard of, such as giant black-and-white bears that ate bamboo (which we now know as pandas), enormous snakes that could swallow animals whole, and "unicorns" that were nothing like the legendary white horses with golden horns—they were actually rhinoceroses! He told of birds so large that they could lift elephants into the sky, a tale likely inspired by the enormous Roc bird from Persian mythology. To people in Venice, these animals sounded like creatures from fairy tales.

Marco also spoke of the incredible wealth of the East. He told of silk, spices, gold, and jewels being traded in enormous marketplaces, where merchants from all over the world gathered. He described cities larger than any in Europe, with wide streets, towering buildings, and intricate canals. He wrote about a system of government so well-organized that the Mongol Empire remained peaceful despite its enormous size. To many Europeans, this sounded too good to be true. How could a land so wealthy and advanced exist when they had never heard of it before?

While some people doubted Marco's stories, there were others who believed him. Merchants, for example, were very interested in what he had to say. Venice was a great trading city, and its merchants were always looking for new goods to sell. If Marco Polo's tales of the riches of the East were true, then there were incredible opportunities waiting for them. Some merchants believed his descriptions of the spice markets of India, the silk trade in China, and the gold mines of the Mongol Empire. They saw his stories as valuable information that could help them find new trade routes and expand their businesses.

Scholars and explorers were also fascinated by Marco's accounts. They saw him as a man who had ventured beyond the known world and returned with knowledge that could change Europe forever. Even if some of his descriptions seemed unbelievable, they still contained valuable details about geography, cultures, and customs that no one else had recorded before.

Despite the mix of doubt and belief, Marco Polo never wavered in his claims. Even when people mocked him, he stood by his words. As he grew older, he continued to tell his stories, refusing to change or exaggerate them further. On his deathbed, when people begged him to admit that he had made up his adventures, Marco simply replied, "I have not told half of what I saw." This statement only added to the mystery—if his book already contained such incredible tales, what other wonders had he witnessed that he had never written down?

Over time, more and more people came to believe Marco Polo. As trade with the East increased, explorers and merchants began to see that his descriptions had been accurate. The world was far bigger than most Europeans had imagined, and Marco Polo had been one of the first to witness it firsthand. His book, *The Travels of Marco Polo*, became one of the most famous books of the Middle Ages. It inspired countless explorers, including Christopher Columbus, who read Marco's book and dreamed of finding a route to the lands described within its pages.

Centuries later, historians would confirm many of Marco's accounts. Archaeological discoveries proved that Kublai Khan's empire was as vast and powerful as he had described. The Chinese inventions he spoke of, such as paper money, gunpowder, and coal, became widely used across the world. The cities he had visited, once thought to be exaggerated, were found to have been just as large and magnificent as he had claimed.

In the end, Marco Polo's journey was not just a story of adventure—it was a story about the power of knowledge. While some doubted him, others listened, learned, and were inspired. His book opened the eyes of Europe to the wonders of the East and helped spark an age of exploration that would change history forever. Even today, people continue to read his tales and wonder what it must have been like to travel the Silk Road, stand before the great Kublai Khan, and see a world that, at the time, was almost completely unknown. Whether doubters or believers, no one can deny that Marco Polo left behind a legacy that continues to shape our understanding of the world.

Chapter 20: The Legacy of a Great Explorer

Marco Polo's journey across the world was one of the most daring adventures in history, but his true legacy did not end when he returned home to Venice. His incredible experiences, carefully recorded in his famous book *The Travels of Marco Polo*, changed the way people saw the world. His tales inspired generations of explorers, merchants, and scholars, paving the way for some of the most important discoveries in history. Even centuries after his death, the influence of Marco Polo's travels can still be felt across the globe. His legacy is not just in the places he visited or the book he wrote—it is in the way he shaped the way people thought about distant lands, trade, exploration, and the vastness of the world itself.

When Marco Polo first returned to Venice, he was not greeted as a hero. After spending more than twenty years in the Mongol Empire, he was seen as a stranger in his own homeland. People struggled to believe his extraordinary stories. They found it hard to imagine that there were lands far richer, larger, and more advanced than Europe. At the time, Venice was one of the most powerful trading cities in the world, and yet Marco described places that seemed far beyond anything the Venetians could comprehend. He spoke of golden palaces, vast cities with millions of people, paper money instead of gold and silver, and incredible inventions that Europeans had never seen before. His descriptions were so detailed and vivid that some people dismissed them as fantasy, while others saw them as valuable knowledge.

Despite the doubt, Marco Polo's book spread across Europe, capturing the imagination of many. His detailed accounts of China, the Silk Road, the Mongol Empire, and the exotic goods of the East helped increase interest in trade. Merchants were fascinated by the spices, silk, and jewels he described, and they sought ways to reach these lands to bring back their riches. His stories helped strengthen the trade networks between Europe and Asia, encouraging merchants to take risks in hopes of discovering new sources of wealth.

Perhaps the greatest impact of Marco Polo's travels was the inspiration he gave to future explorers. More than 200 years after his death, a young Italian sailor named Christopher Columbus read *The Travels of Marco Polo* and was deeply influenced by it. Columbus was fascinated by the descriptions of the riches of the East, and he wanted to find a direct sea route to China and India. He even carried a copy of Marco Polo's book with him on his famous journey across the Atlantic Ocean in 1492. Though Columbus never reached Asia, his voyage led to the discovery of the Americas, changing the course of history forever. Without Marco Polo's writings, Columbus might never have been so determined to seek out unknown lands.

Marco Polo's influence also extended to cartography, the science of mapmaking. Before his journey, European maps of Asia were mostly based on myths, legends, and inaccurate guesses. After Marco Polo returned and shared his knowledge, mapmakers began creating more accurate representations of the lands he had traveled through. His descriptions of cities, rivers, mountains, and trade routes helped European explorers plan their journeys with better knowledge of the lands ahead. Many of the early maps of Asia were based on Marco Polo's accounts, even if some parts contained errors or exaggerations.

Beyond trade and exploration, Marco Polo introduced Europeans to new inventions and ideas from the East. One of the most important things he described was paper money. In China, Kublai Khan had established a system where people used paper instead of gold or silver coins to buy goods. This seemed unbelievable to Europeans at the time, but centuries later, paper currency became the standard form of money in most countries. Marco also wrote about coal, which was used in China as an important source of fuel. While Europeans still relied mostly on wood, Marco's accounts helped spread knowledge about this valuable energy source, which would later become essential during the Industrial Revolution.

Another important part of Marco Polo's legacy is his contribution to the understanding of different cultures. Before his journey, many Europeans had little knowledge of the people of Asia. They thought of the East as a mysterious and distant land, filled with strange customs. Marco Polo's writings gave detailed descriptions of the people he met, their traditions, and the way they lived. He did not simply describe these cultures as strange or inferior—he showed respect for their advancements and explained how they were often more advanced than European societies at the time. This helped change the way people in Europe thought about the rest of the world, breaking down some of the ignorance and misunderstandings that had existed before.

Despite all his contributions, Marco Polo's legacy has been debated for centuries. Some historians have questioned whether he truly traveled to all the places he described. There is little direct evidence that he ever held a high position in Kublai Khan's court, as he claimed. Some believe that he may have exaggerated parts of his story or included details from other travelers he met along the way. However, many of the things he wrote about, such as the Great Wall of China, the use of coal, and the Mongol postal system, were later confirmed to be true. Even if some parts of his story were exaggerated, there is no doubt that he saw and experienced much of what he described.

Over the centuries, Marco Polo's name has become legendary. His journey inspired not only explorers but also writers, artists, and filmmakers. His adventures have been retold in countless books, plays, and movies, keeping his story alive for new generations. His name has even been used in a popular children's game, where one person calls out "Marco!" and others respond with "Polo!"—a playful nod to his legendary travels.

Today, Marco Polo is remembered as one of the greatest explorers in history. His journey took him farther than almost any other

European of his time, and his book opened up a whole new world of possibilities. His tales of adventure, discovery, and exploration continue to inspire those who dream of traveling beyond the horizon, seeking knowledge about places they have never seen. Whether he was a great adventurer, a brilliant storyteller, or a bit of both, there is no doubt that Marco Polo's legacy has endured for more than 700 years.

His travels remind us that the world is vast and full of wonders, waiting to be explored. They show that curiosity and courage can lead to incredible discoveries. Even though centuries have passed since he first set foot on the Silk Road, his story still teaches us an important lesson: there is always more to learn, more to see, and more to discover.

Epilogue

Marco Polo's incredible journey changed the way people saw the world. His stories introduced Europe to lands they had only imagined—great cities, golden palaces, and bustling markets filled with silk, spices, and treasures from the East. Though some doubted his tales, his book inspired explorers for centuries to come.

More than 200 years after Marco Polo's death, another famous traveler, Christopher Columbus, read *The Travels of Marco Polo* and dreamed of finding his own route to Asia. Many believe that Marco's stories helped shape the Age of Exploration, a time when adventurers set sail to uncover the world's hidden wonders.

Today, we still remember Marco Polo as one of history's greatest travelers. His journey was more than just an adventure—it was a bridge between different cultures, proving that the world is full of knowledge, discovery, and endless possibilities. Even now, his fearless spirit encourages explorers, dreamers, and travelers to set out on their own adventures, just as he did so many centuries ago.

The End.